Biblical Ways to Receive Healing

Kenneth E. Hagin

Unless otherwise indicated, all Scripture quotations in this volume are from the *King James Version* of the Bible.

Forth Printing 2006

ISBN-13: 978-0-89276-074-9
ISBN-10: 0-89276-074-5

In the U.S. write:
Kenneth Hagin Ministries
P.O. Box 50126
Tulsa, OK 74150-0126
1-888-28-FAITH
www.rhema.org

In Canada write:
Kenneth Hagin Ministries
P.O. Box 335, Station D,
Etobicoke (Toronto), Ontario
Canada, M9A 4X3
www.rhemacanada.org

Contents

Knowing and Acting On God's Word (Part 1)

Bible Texts: Isaiah 10:27; John 16:13; Mark 11:23,24; Isaiah 53:4,5; Matthew 8:17; 1 Peter 2:24

Central Truth: By putting God's anointed Word in your heart, you can learn to walk in freedom in every area of your life.

When you believe and act upon God's anointed Word, the anointing will break the yoke of bondage and set you free in every area of your life!

ISAIAH 10:27

27 . . . the yoke shall be destroyed because of the anointing.

We often hear it said that it's the anointing that breaks every yoke. But what is a "yoke" in present-day application? A "yoke" is *anything that binds people.* For example, a yoke can be sin, sickness or disease, poverty, or oppression by evil spirits. But, thank God, the yoke shall be destroyed because of the anointing!

My Testimony of Healing

I was sickly until I was seventeen years old. I didn't grow up normally because for the first sixteen years of my life, I couldn't run and play like other children. I played very limitedly because I had a deformed heart and an incurable blood disease. The blood disease made my blood pale orange in color instead of red, and there were other complications. I never had a normal childhood, and about four months before my sixteenth birthday, I became totally bedfast.

Several doctors had been called in on my case. The great Mayo Clinic in Rochester, Minnesota, said one of the doctors on my case was one of the best surgeons in the world. This doctor said that no one in my condition in the history of medical science had ever lived past the age of sixteen.

But, thank God for the Bible, which is God's holy written Word.

The Word is anointed! It's filled with God's power, and God's anointed Word destroys every yoke of bondage, including the yoke of sickness and disease. That's how I was raised up off the bed of sickness — by acting on God's anointed Word.

I had read the Bible as a young Baptist boy, but I didn't know much about acting on the Word. For example, I knew that the Holy Spirit lived inside me. But I didn't know at first that I was supposed *to listen* to Him or that He would guide me to act on God's Word.

JOHN 16:13
13 Howbeit when he, the Spirit of truth, is come, he will GUIDE YOU INTO ALL TRUTH: for he shall not speak of himself; but whatsoever he shall hear, that shall he speak: and he will shew you things to come.

I've thought many times since then that if I had listened to the Holy Spirit sooner, I would not have stayed bedfast for those sixteen months. But I was so busy trying to get someone to help me that I failed to listen to the Holy Spirit on the inside of me. That's where we miss it so many times. Most of us are looking for something in the natural to help us. But if you are saved, the Holy Spirit abides in your spirit, and the Bible says He'll guide you into all truth. God's Word is truth (John 17:17).

'It's All in the Book'

During the time I was bedfast, the Holy Spirit kept trying to tell me I could be healed. Finally one day, I heard something on the inside of me — that still, small voice — say, "You don't have to die at this early age. You can be healed." Well, if I could be healed, I wanted to know *how*. I knew medical science couldn't do anything for me. So I asked the Lord, "*How* can I be healed?" And that same inward voice said, "It's all in the Book."

When I heard the words, "It's all in the Book," I knew the Holy Spirit was talking about the Bible, so I began to diligently study the Bible day and night. When I read Mark 11:23 and 24, those words were branded on my spirit like a branding iron brands cattle.

MARK 11:23,24
23 For verily I [Jesus] say unto you, That whosoever shall say unto this mountain, Be thou removed, and be thou cast into the sea; and shall not doubt in his heart, but shall believe that those things which he saith shall come to pass; he shall have whatsoever he saith.
24 Therefore I say unto you, What things soever ye desire [and that includes healing], when ye pray,

believe that ye receive them, and ye shall have them.

Those words, ". . . *What things soever ye desire, when ye pray, believe that ye receive them, and ye shall have them,*" (v. 24) became indelibly imprinted on my heart. You see, the greatest desire of my heart was to be healed. Nearly sixty-five years ago, as I acted on God's anointed Word, His Word brought healing to my body. And I've been healed ever since!

We've Already Been Redeemed From Sickness!

Healing belongs to us as believers. At the time I was healed, I didn't know about our redemption from sickness and disease. I didn't know about Isaiah 53:4 and 5, and other scriptures about Christ's redemptive work.

ISAIAH 53:4,5
4 Surely he [Jesus] **hath borne our griefs, and carried our sorrows** [the original Hebrew says He bore our sicknesses, and carried our pains]: **yet we did esteem him stricken, smitten of God, and afflicted.**
5 But he was wounded for our transgressions, he was bruised for our iniquities: the chastisement of our peace was upon him; and with his stripes we are healed.

MATTHEW 8:17
17 That it might be fulfilled which was spoken by Esaias [Isaiah] the prophet, saying, Himself [Jesus] took our infirmities, and bare our sicknesses.

1 PETER 2:24
24 Who his own self [Jesus] **bare our sins in his own body on the tree, that we, being dead to sins, should live unto righteousness: by whose stripes ye were healed.**

Many times, this is where folks miss it. They say, "I know God promised to heal me, but He hasn't done it *yet*." This causes folks to become confused. But God didn't promise to heal them *someday*. He said in His Word that they are healed *now*!

To say that God has promised to heal us is like an unsaved person saying, "I know God has promised to save me." No. God didn't *promise* to save the sinner. The Word says that salvation *belongs to every unsaved person right now*! Second Corinthians 5:19 says, ". . . *God was in Christ, reconciling the world unto himself, not imputing their trespasses unto them. . . .*" Salvation is a gift. It was paid for by Jesus Christ. It belongs to us.

Healing belongs to us too! And receiving healing, just like receiving salvation, is simply a matter of appropriating what already belongs to us because of Christ's redemptive work.

Someone said, "Yes, I've read all those wonderful promises in the Word." But these scriptures on healing that we just read are not really promises; they are *statements of fact.* You see, in the mind of God, you're already healed. God has already healed you because He laid sickness and disease on Jesus. Jesus has already borne sickness and disease for you. You need not bear what Jesus already bore for you.

When Isaiah wrote about Jesus' redemptive work, "*Surely he hath borne our griefs, and carried our sorrows . . .*" (Isa. 53:4), he was prophesying about the future. He was looking forward in time to the Cross. Some people say that verse was only prophesying concerning salvation. However, the words "griefs" and "sorrows" are literally translated from the Hebrew as "sickness" and "pain." So our redemption included both remission of sin and physical healing.

When Peter later wrote about Jesus' redemptive work, "*Who his own self bare our sins in his own body on the tree . . . by whose stripes ye were healed*" (1 Peter 2:24), he was looking back in time to the Cross.

Peter wrote, ". . . *by whose stripes ye WERE healed.*" Since you were healed, you *are* healed. In other words, you're not *going to be* healed. You *are* healed! And as you stand in faith on God's Word, your body has to come in line with God's Word, and every symptom has to go!

Someone said, "I just believe God is going to heal me *sometime.*" Well, that's not agreeing with God. In fact, to say that is really taking sides *against* God because God and His Word are one. God's Word is God speaking to us, and God's Word says we *were* healed (1 Peter 2:24)!

Memory Text:
"And ye shall know the truth, and the truth shall make you free."
— John 8:32

Knowing and Acting On the Word (Part 2)

Bible Texts: Matthew 4:4; Romans 10:17; John 8:32

Central Truth: God's Word is anointed. It's filled with God's power to destroy every yoke of bondage, including sickness and disease!

Feed Your Spirit Continually

Some people are always wanting God to speak to them, but if they'd get in the Bible and read it and meditate on it, they'd find that God is speaking to them from every page. They're always looking for some "new" revelation, yet they haven't mastered walking in the light of what they already know. But when you walk in the light of what you know, more light will be given to you. You see, it's the truth of God's anointed Word, not some "new" revelation, that sets people free and destroys every yoke of bondage.

Sometimes when I've tried to read scriptures to people on healing, they've said, "Oh, I've already heard that." That's like a man sitting down at the table to eat, but when a big T-bone steak is put on his plate, he says, "No thanks. I've had T-bone steak before"! Just because you ate a T-bone steak one time doesn't mean you're never going to eat one again!

MATTHEW 4:4

4 ... Man shall not live by bread alone, but by every word that proceedeth out of the mouth of God.

What is this verse saying? It's saying that what natural food is to your body, the Word of God is to your spirit. The Word of God is "food" or nourishment for your spirit. Just because you ate a certain kind of natural food one time doesn't mean you're never going to eat it again. No, you'll come right back to the table and eat the same kinds of food again and again.

5

The Truth Will Set You Free!

When it comes to spiritual things, a preacher can teach on faith and healing and sometimes people say, "Oh, I've heard that before." But in much the same way that we eat the same kind of natural food again and again, we need to come right back to God's table and eat *His* food — the Word of God — again and again.

ROMANS 10:17
17 So then faith cometh by hearing, and hearing by the word of God.

Faith comes by *hearing* and *hearing* the Word of God. In other words, faith doesn't come by hearing it just once or even by hearing it occasionally. The Word of God is anointed and if you get that Word in your heart by hearing it again and again, the anointing will set you free.

JOHN 8:32
32 And ye shall KNOW the truth, and the truth shall make you free.

The truth sets you free. We know that God's Word is truth (John 17:17). The truth of the anointed Word will set you free, but it can't set you free until you *know* it. The way you know the truth is by putting it in your heart — in your spirit. And the way you do that is by hearing the Word continually.

Several years ago, my wife Oretha became physically weak and just kept getting weaker, so she went to have a medical exam. Her doctor discovered a blockage in one side of her heart and immediately ordered more tests. He also told her not to exert herself physically at all. So she spent time in the Word constantly, putting God's medicine — His Word — in her spirit. I have a tape called "Healing Scriptures," and she listened to those healing scriptures almost constantly.

Oretha was scheduled to go back to the doctor for more tests to see whether she would need surgery or if medication alone could help her. One evening before her return visit to the doctor, she was meditating on the Word, thinking about the goodness of God, when she felt something like two hands reach down into her heart and take something out.

She went back to the same doctor for more tests and he couldn't find a thing wrong with her heart! He said the blockage was gone and that her heart was perfectly normal! Her doctor was a Christian, and he said that was the first miracle of that sort he had ever seen. He had seen other people helped through both prayer and medicine, but he had never seen a miracle like hers. What had happened? She just kept putting that Word in her spirit, and God healed her through His anointed Word.

6

You Must Do Your Part

Healing belongs to us, but most folks miss it because they think, *If healing belongs to me, why don't I have it?* In other words, they think the blessings of God are just going to automatically fall on them like ripe cherries fall off a tree. But that's not true. The blessings of God must be *appropriated* by faith in God's written Word. In other words, we must receive by faith the blessings that God has already provided for us in His Word.

The same is true with salvation. For example, have you ever stopped to think about the fact that the new birth, the remission of sin, belongs to the worst sinner, just as much as it belongs to the Christian? The remission of sin belongs to people in jail or prison — even those who are on "death row" — just as much as it belongs to the most faithful churchgoer. Why? Because the Bible says, *"For God so loved THE WORLD, that he gave his only begotten Son, that WHOSOEVER believeth in him should not perish, but have everlasting life"* (John 3:16).

Jesus paid for salvation for every man, woman, boy, and girl who would ever live on this earth. But people must believe on Jesus and receive Him as their own Savior before salvation can benefit them.

So, you see, salvation belongs to the sinner. Then why doesn't every sinner get saved? It's either because no one has told him, so he doesn't know about salvation, or someone has told him about salvation, but he didn't believe it or accept it.

The same thing is true with healing. One reason many Christians haven't received healing is they haven't heard the Word, and they don't know healing belongs to them. They thought they had to stay sick. But healing belongs to them. There are other reasons Christians don't get healed as well, but the point is, healing belongs to them.

We know it's the anointing that destroys every yoke of sickness and disease. But actually, the anointing is released by *acting* on God's anointed Word — that is, by *believing* it and *applying* it to your own life.

It's a Done Deal!

Years ago a crippled woman who hadn't walked in four years attended a meeting I held. She was seventy-two years old and doctors said she would never walk another step. I read Matthew 8:17 and First Peter 2:24 to her. She said, "Yes, I know those scriptures, and I believe them."

I asked her to read aloud the last part of First Peter 2:24, and she read, ". . . *by whose stripes ye were* healed." I said, "Read it again," and she did. Then I asked her, "Is 'were' past tense, present tense, or future tense?"

She looked at me in amazement, and I could see that the light had suddenly dawned on her. She said, "Why, it's past tense. And if we *were* healed, then I *was* healed."

"That's right," I encouraged her. Then I said, "You're still sitting there crippled. You haven't moved a bit. You need to start believing that you *were* healed when the stripes were laid on Jesus. If you believe that, then begin to say, 'If I *was* healed, then I *am* healed.' Start believing you *are* healed *now*."

I talked to this crippled woman about what the Word says, and just kept quoting the Word to her on healing. After about ten minutes, she was leaping and walking and praising God! Some people in that church said, "That Hagin fellow healed a crippled woman in church the other night." But I didn't do any such thing! I can't heal anyone. *Jesus* purchased her healing more than 2,000 years ago. She just found out about it that night!

God's anointed Word will work for you, too, and set you free from every yoke of bondage — sin, sickness or disease, poverty, or anything else the devil tries to bring against you. But you must *act* on God's Word by agreeing with it. You must believe it and feed upon it. That's how you get it into your heart or spirit. As God's Word becomes a part of you, the anointing will deliver you and bring freedom to every area of your life.

✳

Memory Text:

"If ye know these things, happy are ye if ye do them."

— John 13:17

There's Healing Power in The Name of Jesus!

Bible Texts: John 14:12-14; Acts 3:2-8; Philippians 2:9-11; Romans 12:1

Central Truth: Through faith in the Name of Jesus, you can exercise authority over the power of the enemy in your life, and experience deliverance, healing, and victory!

The Name of Jesus belongs to you as a Christian, and you have a right to use that Name. But you need to *know* the power and the authority that's in Jesus' Name, and you must learn to *exercise* that authority.

JOHN 14:12-14
12 Verily, verily, I [Jesus] say unto you, He that believeth on me, the works that I do shall he do also; and greater works than these shall he do; because I go unto my Father.
13 And whatsoever ye shall ask in my name, that will I do, that the Father may be glorified in the Son.
14 If ye shall ask any thing in my name, I will do it.

When we just sort of "skim" over the Word of God, we miss the impact of what the Word is saying. For example, many people believe that

John 14:12-14 is a reference to the subject of prayer. However, a closer examination of this passage will reveal that it is really referring to the believer's right to exercise spiritual authority in the Name of Jesus.

Make a Demand in the Name of Jesus

According to *Strong's Exhaustive Concordance*, the meaning of the Greek word "ask" in John 14:13,14 implies *a demand of something due*. Jesus told the disciples, *"If ye shall ASK [demand] any thing IN MY NAME, I WILL DO IT"* (John 14:14). Jesus was not talking about prayer here; He was talking about using His Name as a basis for authority. And the Early Church used healing as a means of advertising the Gospel as well as a means of blessing and helping people.

ACTS 3:2-8

2 And a certain man lame from his mother's womb was carried, whom they laid daily at the gate of the temple which is called Beautiful, to ask alms of them that entered into the temple;

3 Who seeing Peter and John about to go into the temple asked an alms.

4 And Peter, fastening his eyes upon him with John, said, Look on us.

5 And he gave heed unto them, expecting to receive something of them.

6 Then Peter said, Silver and gold have I none; but such as I have give I thee: IN THE NAME OF JESUS CHRIST of Nazareth rise up and walk.

7 And he took him by the right hand, and lifted him up: and immediately his feet and ankle bones received strength.

8 And he leaping up stood, and walked, and entered with them into the temple, walking, and leaping, and praising God.

Peter didn't demand anything of God when he commanded, "... In the name of Jesus Christ of Nazareth rise up and walk." Why not? Because God never made that man crippled to begin with — Satan did. Peter used the Name of Jesus to set the crippled man free from the bondage of Satan. Peter demanded that the man arise and walk in Jesus' Name!

Later in Acts 3:16, Peter said, "And HIS [Jesus'] NAME through faith in HIS NAME hath made this man strong, whom ye see and know: yea, the faith which is by him hath given him this perfect soundness. . . ." You see, it is that Name — the Name of Jesus — which guarantees the answer!

PHILIPPIANS 2:9-11

9 Wherefore God also hath highly exalted him [Jesus], and given him A NAME WHICH IS ABOVE EVERY NAME:

10 That at THE NAME OF JESUS every knee should bow, of things in heaven, and things in earth, and things under the earth;

11 And that every tongue should confess that Jesus Christ is Lord, to the glory of God the Father.

Other translations of verse 10 say "beings" instead of "things." So we could read verse 10, ". . . every knee should bow, of things [or beings] in heaven, and things [or beings] in earth, and things [or beings] under the earth." Beings in Heaven and earth, and under the earth would include angels and demons. In other words, angels and demons alike are subject to the Name of Jesus. They must surrender to that Name, because the Name of Jesus is superior to every name that can be named!

The Name of Jesus Belongs to You!

As Christians, the Name of Jesus belongs to us. Yet many times, that Name doesn't mean as much to believers as it should because their thinking is wrong. If your thinking is wrong, your believing will be wrong; and if your believing is wrong, then what you say will be wrong too. It all goes back to your thinking. You've got to get your thinking straightened out in order for the Name of Jesus to mean what it should mean to you.

The Bible says, ". . . *faith cometh by hearing, and hearing by the word of God*" (Rom. 10:17). You've got to have *faith* in the Name of Jesus before that Name will produce results for you. When your faith in the Name of Jesus increases, then the results will increase!

Some Christians think of the Name of Jesus in the same way they think of a good luck charm. They have about as much faith in the Name of Jesus as they have in a rabbit's foot! They say, "Maybe it will work," or "I hope something good comes out of it." As long as they just *try* the Name of Jesus like it's some sort of good luck charm — nothing will happen for them, unless God in His mercy intervenes on their behalf and does something for them in spite of themselves.

Using the Name of Jesus To Obtain Healing

The Name of Jesus belongs to you as a Christian, and you have a right to use that Name. When sickness or disease tries to attack you, you can command it to leave your body. That's how I've been able to live for nearly sixty-five years now without having a headache. I didn't say symptoms of a headache never tried to attack me. I said I haven't had a headache in nearly sixty-five years because when a symptom came, I demanded that it leave in Jesus' Name, and it left!

If sickness or disease comes to you, instead of accepting it and talking about your troubles, say, "In the Name of Jesus Christ of Nazareth, leave my body!" And the sickness or disease must go! You may say, "I tried that and it didn't work." Using the Name of Jesus doesn't work by *trying* it; it works by *doing* it! Your spirit man — the real you on the inside — is the ruler of your body. In other words, you are the ruler, or the caretaker of your own body. You are the one who must exercise dominion over it — not someone else.

I once read about a man who was the caretaker of some landscaped property. After repeated efforts to stop people from walking on the grass, this caretaker posted a sign that read: "Gentlemen *will not*, and others *must not* trespass on this property." You see, you — not someone else — are the caretaker of your physical body, and you have a right to forbid Satan to trespass against your body with sickness or disease!

The Apostle Paul said, *"But I keep under my body, and bring it into subjection: lest that by any means, when I have preached to others, I myself should be a castaway"* (1 Cor. 9:27). To bring something into subjection means to rule over something or to take authority over something.

Notice Paul said, "I bring my body into subjection." Some Christians don't bring their bodies into subjection — they are body-ruled. That's what it means to be *carnal*. Yet every Christian has the ability to bring his or her body into subjection, as Paul did. Just because Paul was an apostle, doesn't mean he was any more saved than you are; he didn't have any more authority over his body than you do over yours. But Paul *exercised* his authority. *He* brought his body into subjection.

ROMANS 12:1
1 I beseech you therefore, brethren, by the mercies of God, that ye present your bodies a living sacrifice, holy, acceptable unto God, which is your reasonable service.

Paul addressed the Book of Romans to believers. Romans 1:7 says, *"To all that be in Rome, beloved of God, called to be saints. . . ."* So Romans 12:1 applies to all the beloved of God, called to be saints — whether they are in Rome or in your own hometown. Paul admonished believers: *". . . present your bodies a living sacrifice . . . which is your reasonable service"* (v. 1). One translation says, "which is your spiritual service." Paul said presenting your body to God as a living sacrifice is your spiritual service, and that applies to *every* believer.

You are the ruler of your own body. If you weren't the ruler of your own body, then you couldn't bring it into subjection, and you couldn't present it to God as a living sacrifice according to Romans 12:1. You wouldn't be able to take authority over any sickness or disease that might try to harm you. But you *are* the ruler of your own body, and, thank God, you have a right to freedom from pain, sickness, and disease in the Name of Jesus! But you must exercise the authority which belongs to you *in that Name.*

When you take authority over sickness or disease in your body and command it to leave in Jesus' Name,

12

you are demanding something due you: freedom from whatever it is that has attacked your body. John 14:14 says, *"If ye shall ask* [or demand] *any thing in my name, I will do it."* You're not demanding anything of God; you're demanding something of demon forces because sickness and disease come from the devil, not from God.

Jesus told the disciples to pray, *". . . Thy will be done in earth, as it is in heaven"* (Matt. 6:10). There isn't any sickness in Heaven, and God doesn't want you to be sick here on earth. When you take authority over sickness or disease in your body, you're just taking your place as a child of God with certain rights. You're just exercising your authority and demanding your rights!

Many times, however, Christians will just slip back into the natural, or back into religious thinking which tells them they don't have a say-so about *anything* that happens to them. Rather than *dominating* their circumstances, these Christians are *being dominated* by their circumstances. They have been religiously brainwashed instead of New Testament-taught.

We need to *know* the authority God has given us, *believe* in that authority, and *exercise* it. If we don't know the authority God has given us as we should, we need to meditate upon the Scriptures which tell us who we are in Christ, and the authority which God has given us in the Name of Jesus.

The Name of Jesus won't work just because you saw someone else use it. You must be convinced of the Word of God yourself and then act on the Word because you believe it's true. The Name of Jesus will not work for you as it should until you apply yourself to the study of its meaning and its worth.

When you get the revelation of the power and authority in the Name of Jesus, no one can steal that revelation from you. You must use the Name of Jesus in faith; otherwise, you won't get results. Unbelief cries and begs and pleads, but faith speaks and then shouts the victory!

I didn't get the revelation of that Scripture just by reading it once or twice; I didn't get it by hearing someone else's testimony of how it worked for them. I got the revelation of the power of the Name of Jesus by careful study, meditation, and application of the truth.

Jesus said, *"If ye shall ask* [demand] *any thing in my name, I will do it"* (John 14:14). Someone might say, "Well, I don't know about that. I *tried* using the Name of Jesus once and it didn't work." Once the reality of the authority that's in the Name of Jesus has dawned on you —

once the authority that's in the Name of Jesus has become a reality in your spirit — your days of *trying* are over and your days of *doing* will begin!

Every believer should clearly understand the power and authority in the Name of Jesus and the believer's right to use that Name. Meditate upon the Scriptures that tell you who you are in Christ and what authority you have as a believer. As you do, those Scriptures will become a reality to you. And you will begin to exercise your right to perfect deliverance from the bondage of Satan — for yourself and for your loved ones — in the Name of Jesus!

✳

Memory Text:
*"And his [Jesus'] name
through faith in his name
hath made this man strong,
whom ye see and know: yea,
the faith which is by him
hath given him this perfect
soundness in the presence
of you all."*
— Acts 3:16

Prayer for Healing

Bible Texts: John 16:23,24; Matthew 18:19,20.

Central Truth: Prayer is successful only when it is based on the promises in God's Word!

The Bible teaches that there are several kinds of prayer. However, I will not go into detail on all of them in this lesson. (I do have several books on prayer which discuss them in more detail.) Right now I just want to concentrate on prayer for healing.

Pray to the Father in the Name of Jesus

JOHN 16:23,24
23 And IN THAT DAY ye shall ask me nothing. Verily, verily, I say unto you, Whatsoever ye shall ask the Father IN MY NAME, he will give it you.
24 Hitherto have ye asked nothing IN MY NAME: ask, and ye shall receive, that your joy may be full.

What day was Jesus talking about when He said "... *in that day ye shall ask me nothing...*" (v. 23)? He was talking about the day that we are living in right now. Praying to the Father in the Name of Jesus belongs to us *now* — in this day.

Jesus said that just before He went to Calvary to die, be raised from the dead, ascend on high, and sit at the right hand of the Father. At that time, a new day dawned, and we came into the *New Covenant*.

Notice John 16:24 says, *"Hitherto have ye asked nothing in my name..."* The word "hitherto" means *until now*. Jesus was really saying, "Until this time you have not prayed in My Name." It wouldn't have done the disciples or anyone else any good to have prayed to the Father in the Name of Jesus while Jesus was here on earth, because, under the *Old*

Covenant, they prayed to the God of Abraham, Isaac, and Jacob.

You see, when Jesus was here on earth, He had not yet entered His mediatory (high priestly or intercessory) ministry at the right hand of the Father, so it would not have done any good to have prayed in His Name.

But just before He went away, Jesus changed His disciples' way of praying. During the interim when the Old Covenant was going out and the New Covenant was coming in, Jesus taught the disciples to pray what we call "The Lord's Prayer" (Matt. 6:9). He did not teach *us* to pray this way; He taught His *disciples* to pray this way.

I did not say The Lord's Prayer isn't beautiful. I did not say we cannot learn something from it — because we can learn much from it. But where is the Name of Jesus in it? The disciples didn't pray one thing in the Name of Jesus, did they? They didn't ask for one thing in the Name of Jesus. *This is not the New Testament Church at prayer!* This is not the New Testament model for prayer.

There's something we need to take note of in John chapter 16: Just before Jesus went away, He changed the disciples' way of praying. *Under the New Covenant between God and the Church, we are to come to God by Jesus Christ.* One reason we have

missed a great deal is that we have tried to pray as they did back in the days of the Old Covenant.

Notice Jesus said, "*. . . ASK and ye SHALL RECEIVE, that your joy may be full*" (v. 24). Of course, this includes all prayer, but it includes praying for healing as well. How could your joy be full if you or your loved ones were home sick? That would be impossible, wouldn't it?

If we were getting more answers to prayer, we would have more joy. And if more of our joy were showing, we would get more people saved and healed.

Healing is involved in these verses. We have a right to ask for healing in the Name of Jesus. God does hear and answer prayer.

Agree in Prayer

MATTHEW 18:19,20
19 Again I [Jesus] say unto you, That if two of you shall agree on earth as touching any thing that they shall ask, it shall be done for them of my Father which is in heaven.
20 For where two or three are gathered together in my name, there am I in the midst of them.

Frequently we take verse 20 out of its setting and apply it only to church services — but that really isn't what it's talking about. You see, verses 19 and 20 go together. According to verse

16

20, wherever two people are, agreeing in prayer, Jesus is there to see that what they agreed upon happens. Jesus is not talking about a church meeting here, although He *is* present in church meetings.

Where two people are united and are demanding healing for themselves or their loved ones in Jesus' Name, their prayers are bound to be answered, because God watches over His Word to make it good (Jer. 1:12)! Matthew 18:19 says "two of you on earth," not "two of you in Heaven." Just two. And the phrase "anything that they shall ask" could include healing, couldn't it?

Well, the "two of you" could be husband and wife. My wife and I have had marvelous answers to prayer by agreeing together. Yet people tell me, "Brother Hagin, we *tried* that, and it didn't work." My wife and I didn't *try*. We *did* it! Jesus didn't say that two should *try* to agree; He said to *do* it.

Sometimes we get into the natural and think, *Now, if I could get enough people — maybe a thousand — agreeing; maybe ten thousand praying, that would really get results!* That is human reasoning. God said that *two could get the job done.* Two is the most that He ever mentions are needed! He didn't say to get the whole church to agree on it. (You couldn't get a whole church

to agree on something to save your life!) But if two of you agree, that's all it takes.

Jesus said, "*. . . if two of you shall agree on earth as touching any thing . . . IT SHALL BE . . .*" (v. 19). Jesus didn't say it might be or it's a possibility. He said, "*. . . IT SHALL BE DONE for them of my Father which is in heaven.*"

Often people ask me to agree with them in prayer for financial, physical, and spiritual needs. I usually join hands with them and pray: "We are joining hands here physically to denote the fact that our spirits are agreeing. We agree that this need *is* met — not that it is going to be, because that is not faith, that would be future tense. That would be hope, not faith. We agree that the need is met, so we are praising God because we have agreed that it shall be done. By faith it is done right now, and we count it as done."

After praying like this, I ask the person, "Is it done?"

Eight times out of ten the person starts bawling, "Brother Hagin, I *hope* it is."

I have to tell them, "It isn't. I'm *believing* and you're *hoping*. There is no agreement here. It didn't work."

There is no use in our going around blaming God and casting bad reflections on the Bible if it didn't work. Friends, if it didn't work, *we* didn't work it, because Jesus Christ cannot lie! We must admit that we didn't do it and then correct ourselves.

Add Praise to Your Prayers and Get Results!

When I tell people they don't have to pray to be healed, they look at me in amazement. Many have failed to receive healing because they have based their faith on prayer instead of on God's Word. They expected prayer to do for them what God's Word will do for them. But prayer is successful only when it is based on the promises in God's Word!

It seems that most of our prayers are prayers of petition — asking God to do something for us. And, of course, it's scriptural for us to pray that way, but we also need to add praise to our prayers, because it's in that kind of atmosphere that God can move more readily in our midst.

A young Pentecostal evangelist found that out when he was dying of tuberculosis back in the early 1930s. He told me his story firsthand.

He had become bedfast and was hemorrhaging from both lungs. He had had to take his family to live on his father-in-law's farm.

One day his father-in-law was out in the fields plowing and his wife and mother-in-law were behind the house doing the wash. So this young evangelist begged God for enough strength to get out of bed and make it to a clump of trees and bushes a quarter of a mile down the road. He purposed in his heart, *I'm going to pray until I pray through and God heals me, or until they find me dead* — *one of the two.*

He reached the thicket and fell down exhausted. He couldn't have cried for help if he had wanted to. No one knew where he was.

"They won't find you until the buzzards lead them to you," the devil assured him.

"Well," the evangelist said, "that's all right, devil. That's why I came out here. Just as soon as I can regain a little strength, I'm going to pray until I'm healed or die at this spot."

The young man said, "As I was lying there, trying to muster enough strength to start praying, I got to thinking about it: Everywhere I had been, I had turned in prayer requests for my healing. *Hundreds* of people had prayed. *Thousands* of people had prayed. Every healing evangelist in America had laid hands on me. *Everybody* had prayed.

"If you put all those prayers together, it would add up to hundreds of hours of prayer. Many great men of faith had laid hands on me —

18

and God uses healing evangelists. I finally decided, 'I'm not going to pray at all. There is no use in my praying. I see where I've missed it. I shouldn't even have turned in all those prayer requests. I've been trying to get a bunch of people to pray for me. I've been trying to get God to give me what He said is already mine!'

"The Bible says I'm healed. So, Lord, I'm going to lie here flat on my back and praise You. I'm going to praise You until my healing is manifested."

That young evangelist told me, "I just started whispering, 'Praise the Lord. Glory to God. Hallelujah. Thank You, Jesus.' After about ten minutes of whispering, I got enough strength to lift my arms up by propping my elbows on the ground. And I praised God for another ten minutes or so. Then I got enough strength to lift my hands, and my voice got louder. At the end of two hours, I was on my feet hollering, 'Praise God,' so loudly that someone heard me several miles away!"

You see, when he began to agree with what the Word of God says and acted on God's Word, he got results!

Memory Text:
"*. . . the prayer of faith shall save the sick . . . pray one for another, that ye may be healed.*
The effectual fervent prayer of a righteous man availeth much."
— James 5:15,16

The Laying On of Hands (Part 1)

Bible Texts: Hebrews 6:1,2; Exodus 29:10,15,19; Deuteronomy 34:9; Acts 13:2,3

Central Truth: The laying on of hands is a fundamental principle of the doctrine of Christ.

The Doctrine of Christ

A Pentecostal minister once told me: "Twenty-five years ago, God spoke to me about a ministry of laying on of hands, but I backed off from it. Even though God used me in it, some of the brethren didn't understand it, and I didn't want to make a doctrine out of it."

"You didn't have to," I said. "Jesus made a doctrine out of it."

HEBREWS 6:1,2
1 Therefore leaving the principles of the doctrine of Christ, let us go on unto perfection; not laying again the foundation of repentance from dead works, and of faith toward God,
2 Of THE DOCTRINE of baptisms, and OF LAYING ON OF HANDS, and
of resurrection of the dead, and of eternal judgment.

"Laying on of hands" is one of the six fundamental principles of the doctrine of the Lord Jesus Christ listed in Hebrews 6:1-2. Those principles are:

1. *Repentance* — This leads to the New Birth experience.

2. *Faith toward God* — The Bible says we can't be saved without faith: "... *by grace are ye saved through faith; and that not of yourselves: it is the gift of God: Not of works, lest any man should boast*" (Eph. 2:8-9).

3. *Doctrine of Baptisms* — Notice this is in the plural. There are three baptisms spoken of in the New Testament. First, there is the New Birth. When a person is born again,

he is baptized by the Holy Spirit into the Body of Christ. Second, there is water baptism, which is an outward sign of an inward grace. Third, there is the baptism in the Holy Spirit with the Bible evidence of speaking in other tongues.

4. *Laying on of Hands* — We will examine this doctrine later.

5. *Resurrection of the Dead* — Notice Hebrews 6:2 does not say "the" resurrection. It says, ". . . *and of resurrection of the dead . . .*" Had it said "the resurrection," there would be just one resurrection; but there is more than one resurrection, so it says "resurrection of the dead."

This includes the first resurrection, the second resurrection, and all other resurrections. It includes the fact that the dead in Christ shall be raised first; then we who are alive and remain at the coming of Christ will be caught up, too (this is the rapture of the saints).

6. *Eternal Judgment* — Again, it is not "the" doctrine of "the" eternal judgment; it is simply doctrine "of eternal judgment." This is because there is more than one judgment, and all are involved in this doctrine.

If I were to say, "I don't much believe in the New Birth, water baptism, or the baptism in the Holy Spirit," you'd be ready to quit me right now, and I wouldn't blame you.

And you would be certain something was wrong with me if I were to say, "I don't think the dead will ever be resurrected." Or "I don't go along with this judgment business. I don't think there's going to be any judgment."

You would say, "There's something wrong with that fellow. He's not solid. He doesn't believe the fundamental principles of the doctrine of Christ."

Well, no matter what else we believe, we must believe the fundamentals. I can fellowship with anyone who believes the fundamentals.

The Doctrine of Laying On of Hands

The Bible has a great deal to say about the doctrine of laying on of hands. That's why it's surprising to me that some Christians see no significance at all in this scriptural ordinance and doctrine. Some regard it with something like astonishment. Others regard it with fear. But the laying on of hands is one of the half-dozen fundamental principles of the doctrine of the Lord Jesus Christ!

I have even heard Full Gospel ministers say, "I don't much go along with the laying on of hands." To deny one of the fundamental principles of the doctrine of Jesus Christ is a serious matter.

Actually, laying on of hands is a theme that runs through the entire Bible. Here are two examples from the Old Testament:

EXODUS 29:10,15,19
10 And thou [Moses] shalt cause a bullock to be brought before the tabernacle of the congregation: and Aaron and his sons shall PUT THEIR HANDS UPON the head of the bullock. . . .
15 Thou shalt also take one ram; and Aaron and his sons shall put their hands upon the head of the ram. . . .
19 And thou shalt take the other ram; and Aaron and his sons shall put their hands upon the head of the ram.

We read here that the *imperfections* of the worshippers were transferred by faith to the sacrifice. The sacrifice was a type of Christ. The *perfections* of the sacrifice were received by faith by the man who laid hands on the sacrifice. It was God's power that effected the two-way transmission.

The Book of Deuteronomy tells us that Joshua had the same spirit of wisdom that Moses had because Moses had laid his hands upon him. This implies that whatever Moses had was transferred to Joshua by the laying on of hands.

DEUTERONOMY 34:9
9 And Joshua the son of Nun was full of the spirit of wisdom; FOR MOSES HAD LAID HIS HANDS UPON HIM: and the children of Israel hearkened unto him, and did as the Lord commanded Moses.

Today through the ordinance of laying on of hands, God's power is transmitted by faith through the minister to the seeker.

As far as I know, most churches practice the laying on of hands to some extent. The most common practice is laying hands on those who are being ordained and separated unto the ministry. Something mighty occurs when men of faith lay hands in the Name of the Lord upon those who, by faith, receive the impartation. There is scriptural precedent for this.

ACTS 13:2,3
2 As they ministered to the Lord, and fasted, the Holy Ghost said, Separate me Barnabas and Saul for the work whereunto I have called them.
3 And when they had fasted and prayed, and laid their hands on them, they sent them away.

The doctrine of laying on of hands does not end with the ordination of ministers, however, as so many denominations believe. That is only one facet of laying on of hands.

Some churches also believe in laying hands on those being installed in certain church offices. Again, there is scriptural precedent for this. In Acts 6, seven men were selected to wait on tables, freeing the apostles to give themselves continually to prayer and the ministry of the Word. The apostles laid their hands on the seven, who were called deacons — "helpers" in the Greek.

Laying on of hands is not limited to ordinations, however. In nearly every instance in the Acts of the Apostles where people were filled with the Holy Spirit, they received *by the laying on of hands.* (Exceptions were the spontaneous outpourings of the Spirit in Acts 2 and Acts 10.) But in Acts 8:17, when Peter and John laid their hands on Philip's Samaritan converts, they received the Holy Spirit. And in Acts 19:6, Paul laid hands on the disciples at Ephesus, and *". . . they spake with tongues, and prophesied."*

Of course people can be filled with the Spirit in other ways, but the laying on of hands is one scriptural method.

Laying Empty Hands
On Empty Heads

I realize that there is an unprofitable kind of laying on of hands. There are extremes of this practice in the church world.

One extreme is a mere ritual. There are churches that have a ritual of laying hands on people to confirm them. According to some church creeds, one receives the Holy Spirit at this time. But because this is a mere ritual and formality, usually nothing happens.

On the other hand, there have been extremes even in Full Gospel circles. People have had hands laid on them for nearly everything you could mention — and some you couldn't.

For example, a woman told me that she went to a meeting where hands were laid on her. She was prophesied over, and she supposedly was given "the gift of casting out permanent waves." I told her if she could have gotten the gift of putting them in, she would have had something!

Once a man came up to me after a service several years ago and asked, "Brother Hagin, could you help me?"

I said, "I'll be glad to if I can."

He told me he had been in a meeting where someone laid hands on him and gave him the gifts of healing, the gift of the word of knowledge, and two or three other spiritual gifts. He said, "I can see that these things are manifested in your ministry. Maybe you could tell me how to operate them. I know I've got them, because that fellow said I did."

I asked, "How long has it been since hands were laid on you?"

"Well," he said, "over six months ago."

I said, "Has there ever been any kind of manifestation?"

"Not that I know of," he replied.

I said, "I'd forget it if I were you. You don't have anything. If it's there, it would rise to the surface."

Then in another place I preached, a woman sat on the second pew, right in front of the pulpit, and rocked just like she was in a rocking chair throughout my sermon. I thought the poor dear was afflicted with some kind of serious physical ailment.

Afterwards I asked the pastor, "What's wrong with that woman? People were looking at her. She was distracting from the message."

"Oh," the pastor said, "Brother Hagin, that's a sad case. There's nothing wrong with her physically. She's not a member here, but she does come to church some. I've been intending to talk to her about it, but I just haven't had time. She attended a meeting somewhere, and someone laid hands on her and gave her 'the gift of rocking.'"

Several nights later that woman came up to me after the service accompanied by a woman who had told her there is nothing in the Bible about "the gift of rocking."

She said, "Brother Hagin, explain my gift to this woman."

Well, I thought that would be a good opportunity for the pastor to talk to her! I said, "I'm on my way out of the building. You talk with the pastor of this church. He's a man of God and knows the Bible quite well. He'll be glad to help you."

Afterwards, the pastor said, "You dog!"

I said, "Well, you *said* you wanted to talk to her, so I arranged it. Were you able to help her?"

He said, "Certainly not. No one could help her."

I asked, "Well, what did she tell you? What is the purpose of this so-called gift?"

The pastor answered, "She said that God had given it to her so the pastor or the guest speaker could tell when things were in the Spirit. If she is rocking when we're singing, testifying, or preaching, then everything is in the Spirit."

I know this sounds ridiculous, but it is true. I'm not making it up.

I call all these examples *laying empty hands on empty heads.*

I am not going to be frightened out of a New Testament practice, however, because of fanaticism, nor am I going to be frozen out because of formality. The real is not done away with because of excesses. I'm going to

practice the New Testament doctrine
of laying on of hands and it's going to
produce New Testament results!

Memory Text:

*"And he [Jesus] cometh to
Bethsaida; and they bring a
blind man unto him, and
besought him to touch him."*

— Mark 8:22

The Laying On of Hands (Part 2)

Bible Texts: Mark 6:5; 8:22-25; 7:32,33-35; 5:22,23; Acts 19:11,12

Central Truth: Every Christian should practice the doctrine of laying on of hands on the sick, because Jesus said we should!

As I said in the previous lesson, we can't stop practicing the New Testament doctrine of laying on of hands just because some people fall into a ditch on one side or the other. We need to study the New Testament carefully to see how Jesus and the apostles practiced this doctrine.

The Example of Jesus and the Apostles

Jesus Christ Himself freely employed laying on of hands in healing people. In Mark 6, we see Jesus in His hometown of Nazareth:

MARK 6:5
5 And he could there do no mighty work, save that HE LAID HIS HANDS UPON A FEW SICK FOLK, AND HEALED THEM.

Notice this text is speaking of the Lord Jesus Christ Himself — the Son of God. It doesn't say He *wouldn't* do mighty works in Nazareth; it says He *couldn't*. It seems, therefore, that the laying on of hands will work when nothing else will! The few who were healed that day were healed by the laying on of Jesus' hands.

There are several accounts of Jesus' laying hands on people in the New Testament. Matthew 8:15 says that when Jesus entered Peter's house, He found Peter's mother-in-law sick with a fever. *"And he touched her hand, and the fever left her: and she arose, and ministered unto them."* Let's look at a few more examples.

MARK 8:22-25
22 And he [Jesus] cometh to Bethsaida; and they bring a blind man unto him, AND BESOUGHT HIM TO TOUCH HIM.

23 And he took the blind man by the hand, and led him out of the town; and when he had spit on his eyes, AND PUT HIS HANDS UPON HIM, he asked him if he saw ought.

24 And he looked up, and said, I see men as trees, walking.

25 After that HE PUT HIS HANDS AGAIN UPON HIS EYES, and made him look up: and he was restored, and saw every man clearly.

Praise God, the blind man was healed by the laying on of Jesus' hands. Some will say, "Jesus prayed for that blind man twice." I do not know that He prayed for him at all, for the Bible does not say He prayed. The Bible says H*e laid hands on him twice*! Therefore, it is scripturally correct to lay your hands a second time on a sick person, if necessary. It is good to know what Jesus did in certain circumstances. Then we will know what to do.

MARK 7:32,33,35

32 And they bring unto him [Jesus] one that was deaf, and had an impediment in his speech; and they beseech him to PUT HIS HAND UPON HIM.

33 And he took him aside from the multitude, and put his fingers into his ears, and he spit, and touched his tongue. . . .

35 And straightway his ears were *opened, and the string of his tongue was loosed,* and he spake plain.

In the case of the deaf man, the Scriptures do not say that the people asked Jesus to heal the man, although it is implied. It says they asked Him to put His hands on him.

In the above two cases, notice that groups of people brought the blind man and the deaf man to Jesus. These people, as well as the sick themselves, believed in the laying on of hands — and they got results!

If you want the laying on of hands to work for you, you've got to believe in it. You see, without faith, the laying on of hands is a mere ritual, and nothing happens.

Mark chapter 5 tells us that Jairus, a ruler of the synagogue in Galilee, also believed in the laying on of hands.

MARK 5:22,23

22 And, behold, there cometh one of the rulers of the synagogue, Jairus by name; and when he saw him [Jesus], he fell at his feet,

23 And besought him greatly, saying, My little daughter lieth at the point of death: I pray thee, come and LAY THY HANDS ON HER, that she may be healed; and she shall live.

You see, Jairus believed in the laying on of hands. He didn't say, "Come and *pray* for her." He didn't even say, "Come and *heal* her." He said, "*Come and lay thy hands on her that she may be healed.*" Jairus believed his daughter would be healed when hands were laid on her.

We know from Scripture that the child had died before Jesus reached Jairus' house, but verse 41 says, "*. . . he took the damsel by the hand. . . .*" In other words, Jesus touched her. He took her by the hand and she was raised from the dead healed (v. 42)!

Jesus laid hands on sick people, and He exhorted believers to lay hands on the sick too. In Mark 16:18 Jesus said, "*. . . they [believers] shall lay hands on the sick, and they shall recover.*"

Who shall lay hands on the sick? It's not just the preacher. The answer is in Mark 16:15-18, where Jesus declared, "*. . . Go YE into all the world, and preach the gospel to every creature. . . . And these signs shall follow THEM THAT BELIEVE; In my name. . . . they shall lay hands on the sick, and they shall recover.*"

People still preach repentance and water baptism. No one objects to that. Well, why not preach all of The Great Commission? Why stop with just part of it? Why not preach the laying on of hands? Laying on of hands is part of The Great Commission too!

The disciples obviously took Jesus seriously. Acts 5:12 says, "*And by the hands of the apostles were many signs and wonders wrought among the people. . . .*"

In Acts 28:8 and 9 we find the Apostle Paul shipwrecked on an island. The father of the ruler of the island was ill, so Paul went to his house "*. . . and prayed, and laid his hands on him, and healed him.*" The man was healed by the laying on of hands. Then the Bible tells us that the islanders brought their sick to Paul, and Paul ministered to them. Obviously, Paul ministered by the laying on of hands.

ACTS 19:11,12
11 And God wrought special miracles BY THE HANDS OF PAUL:
12 So that from his body were brought unto the sick handkerchiefs or aprons, and the diseases departed from them, and the evil spirits went out of them.

Not only were the sick healed, but the demon-oppressed were delivered as cloths Paul had laid his hands on were laid upon their bodies. These cloths were anointed with the same *power* Paul was anointed with. When we talk about anointed cloths, however, we do not mean cloths anointed with oil.

God wrought special miracles by the hands of Paul (v. 11). Paul laid his hands upon the cloths. God uses men's hands. He works through men's hands.

Some will say, "The apostles could do that, but it is not for us today." It seems to me that intelligent people should have caught on to that worn-out lie by now. Jesus didn't say these signs would follow just the apostles. To say that we cannot lay hands on the sick today is to say that one of the fundamental principles of the doctrine of Christ has been done away with. And if laying on of hands for healing has been done away with, no one would have a right to believe in the doctrine of repentance.

But I'm not going to take anything away from the doctrine of Christ. I believe all of it. I am a follower of Christ. I am a stickler for the doctrine of Christ. And one of the doctrines of Christ is laying on of hands.

'These Signs Shall Follow'

As I said before, Jesus did not say these signs shall follow just the apostles, the preachers, or the teachers. He said, ". . . *these signs shall follow them that believe . . ."* (Mark 16:17).

When I was a Baptist boy, I knew nothing about divine healing, for I had never heard it preached. I just knew what Mark 11:22-24 says about faith and prayer.

My body was almost totally paralyzed. I had a serious organic heart condition and an incurable blood disease. The doctors said I had to die, but I prayed the prayer of faith for myself and was healed. I came off that deathbed as a Baptist boy who preached faith and healing. I didn't know anyone else who believed in divine healing, but it never bothered me.

I stood on the Word of God and said, "Come hell or high water, I'm standing on it. Nobody's going to move me off it!"

One day back in 1935, a Presbyterian woman told me her Pentecostal mother-in-law was coming for a visit. "You'll be interested in meeting Grandma," she said, "because she believes like you do. She believes in divine healing."

She told me how her eighty-two-year-old mother-in-law got people healed while visiting them in their homes and laying hands on them. What a healing ministry this elderly Pentecostal woman had!

I never was so thrilled in my life to finally meet someone who had enough sense to believe the Bible! I knew she was arriving on a certain day, so I went over late that afternoon. After I was introduced, I said to this dear old lady, "Grandma, tell me your story."

"Well," she said, "we came out here to Texas many, many years ago (about 1865). My dad settled on some land that was forty miles to the nearest school, so I didn't go. I didn't get any education.

"I grew up, married a neighbor boy whose folks also owned a lot of land, and we had our family. I still didn't know how to read or write, but I sent our children to school. They were all grown when some people came along and started what they called a brush arbor meeting. They put up some posts, strung some wires from post to post, and put brush on top of it. I got saved and baptized with the Holy Ghost during that meeting.

"When I got baptized with the Holy Ghost and spoke with other tongues, God taught me to read the Bible. I can read the Bible and never make a mistake, but it's all I can read. I can't read anything else.

"Then we moved to town. My husband and the boys would go out to work the farm in the daytime, and I'd be left alone. I got to asking the Lord, 'Lord, is there something I can do? I couldn't sing in the church, because I didn't have a voice for music. I couldn't teach a Sunday school class because they used a quarterly, and I couldn't read the quarterly.

"One day I was at home praying and reading the Book of Mark in the Bible, and I read, '. . . *these signs shall follow them that believe. . . . they shall lay hands on the sick, and they shall recover.*' And I thought, *It doesn't take any education to lay hands on folks.*

"It says believers will lay hands on the sick. So I just went through the neighborhood and inquired about any sick folk I could find. I would spend from nine in the morning until three in the afternoon every day visiting sick people and reading the Bible to them on the subject of healing. Usually they had never heard about it.

"After reading to them about three days, I would ask, 'Now would you like for me to lay hands on you?' You know, practically everybody I laid hands on got healed! The amazing thing about it is that most of the people I was laying hands on were bedfast and given up to die by the doctors."

Here was a little uneducated woman who wasn't a minister of the Gospel — she had never even taught a Sunday school class — but she was laying hands on the sick and they were recovering!

Laying on of hands belongs to all of us. Remember now, this dear old lady was not a preacher; but she was a believer. God is the same God now as He was then. He hasn't changed. And when He finds someone He can work with, God and man can do it again.

Who can lay hands on the sick? *Believers* can!

Methods

Laying on of hands can be done in two ways:

First, any believer can lay hands upon a fellow believer as a point of contact to release faith and expect that person to be healed.

There are some people — friends and neighbors, for example — you can pray for whom no one else could. It also is scriptural for husbands and wives to lay hands on each other and for parents to lay hands on their children when they are sick, and expect them to be healed in the Name of Jesus.

Second, there is such a thing as a *ministry of laying on of hands* — a special anointing. As God wills, a person can be supernaturally anointed with healing power like Jesus or Paul.

When the person who has a ministry of laying on of hands lays hands on the sick in obedience to the spiritual law of contact and transmission, his hands transmit God's healing power into the body of the sick person, effecting a healing and a cure. I explain this method further in another lesson.

Memory Text:
"And these signs shall follow them that believe;
In my name. . . . they shall lay hands on the sick, and they shall recover."
— Mark 16:17,18

Faith and Power — Two Ingredients for Receiving Healing

Bible Texts: Acts 10:38; Mark 5:25-34

Central Truth: The supernatural healing power of God will operate effectively in your life when you understand the laws that govern it and learn to use your faith to activate God's power!

We need to realize that there is no set way by which people may receive healing. In other words, a number of methods for receiving healing are recorded in the Word of God.

One way you can receive healing is by what I call *simple faith* — when you hear the Word of God yourself, believe that what it says is true, and receive your healing by faith in God's Word.

A second way is *to be ministered to with the laying on of hands* — the healing anointing flows through another person to you.

A third way to receive healing is in conjunction with what older Pentecostals often called, *"praying the power down"* — receiving your healing when the supernatural power of God is manifested upon you.

All of these methods are scriptural, all of them require faith, and, thank God, all of them work! In the next few lessons, we are going to discuss these three methods, with our main focus on the two ingredients which are required for each of them to work — *faith and power*.

The Healing Power of God

Concerning the power, Acts 10:38 indicates that the terms "the anointing," "the Holy Ghost," and "power" are virtually synonymous. This means that we are able to use these terms interchangeably when discussing the subject of the healing anointing and the power of God.

A good analogy for understanding the anointing or the power of God was made by the late Rev. John G.

Lake when he said, *"Electricity is God's power in the natural realm; Holy Ghost power is God's power in the spirit realm."*

You see, just as electricity is in existence in the natural world, the power of God is in existence in the spirit world. And just as there are laws that govern the operation of electricity in the natural realm, there are also laws that govern the operation of spiritual power. The problem has been that in times past, we have thought that if the anointing was present, it would automatically manifest itself and just work automatically. That's just not so.

For example, electricity has been in existence in the earth since God created the universe. But did that electricity just automatically light up a house, cook a meal, or warm or cool a house? No, because for many years, man didn't even know electricity existed.

Even after electricity was discovered and man knew it existed, it didn't automatically begin to operate. Man had to come in contact with it somehow to make it work.

Well, if we could just get into our minds the fact that the healing power of God is in existence in the spirit world and that it also has laws that govern its operation, then men and women could learn to tap into

that power and be blessed by its benefits.

I've heard people ask, "If the power of God to heal exists, why doesn't it just move on our behalf?"

That's where we've missed it. We've thought, *Well, if it's so, it'll just manifest itself.*

But, no, there's something that has to be done on man's end before there will be a manifestation of the healing power.

In the natural, there came a time when man knew about electricity; it had even been manifested in a measure. But man had to learn more about electricity and the laws that governed it before he could fully enjoy it — before he could gain the greatest benefit from it.

It's the same way with God's power — the anointing. That simply means that as we learn more about the anointing and what the Word of God says about it, we will be able to flow with the anointing, tap into the power, and gain greater benefits from it.

The Switch of Faith

Now that we understand something about the power of God as "heavenly electricity," as it were, let's extend the analogy a step further concerning faith. Another thing about the laws that govern this heavenly substance is this fact: The thing that turns the heavenly power on in the spiritual realm can be compared to an electrical switch on a wall that turns on the earthly power — electricity — in the natural realm.

In the natural, when you turn a light switch on, electricity flows right into the lighting fixtures and lights up the room. When you turn the switch off, the lights go out. So in the spiritual realm, the thing that turns on the heavenly power could be called the *switch of faith!*

Remember Jesus said to the woman with the issue of blood, *". . . Daughter, THY FAITH hath made thee whole . . ."* (Mark 5:34). Jesus said that her faith had made her whole. In other words, she had turned on the switch of faith for healing and activated the power of God!

When I was a teenager, I was bedfast for sixteen months with an incurable blood disease. Beside my bed was an electrical outlet. Anyone could have plugged a light in there, and it would have lit up the room. The electricity was there, but there was no manifestation of it whatsoever because no one had plugged anything into the outlet.

Well, by the same token, the power of God to heal was present in my room every single day, because God is everywhere present, and whatever power He has is with Him!

But there was no manifestation of it. Why not? Because I didn't plug in to it! I didn't know how!

But, you see, on the eighth day of August, 1934, I learned how. *By faith, I plugged into God's power to heal!* And I began to say, "Now I believe I'm well."

If a man believes he's well, then he'll act like he's well. Even though I was paralyzed, I had regained some use of the upper part of my body, so I pushed my feet off the bed. They fell to the floor like a couple of chunks of wood. I could look down there and see that they were down there on the floor, but I couldn't *feel* them. I was "dead" from my waist down. Then I managed to get hold of one of the bedposts and scoot my body off the bed. I wrapped my arms around that post, but my knees sagged to the floor.

Out loud, I said, "I want to announce in the Presence of Almighty God, the Lord Jesus Christ, the holy angels, and the devil and all of his cohorts that according to the Word of God, I am healed!"

Now when I said that, I "plugged in." I felt that power strike me in the top of my head and ooze down all over me. It felt like someone was above me pouring a pitcher of warm honey on me. It went down my body and my arms. When it got to my waist and down my legs, it felt like ten thousand pins were sticking in my legs. It felt so bad, I could have cried if it hadn't felt so good at the same time! When you have had no feeling at all, it feels good to feel *anything*!

After that happened, I was standing up straight! Hallelujah! I plugged in to that power. *You can plug in to God's power on your own faith!*

Now you can teach people the Word, and they can believe God's Word and receive healing. I was healed as a young boy by simply believing and acting upon God's Word.

However, not everyone is at the level in his faith where he can just believe God's Word for himself and receive healing through faith in the Word alone. Therefore, we should endeavor to teach and preach all of it — every side of divine healing — and to minister to people on all levels of faith and by all methods of healing.

Faith in the Anointing

Let's look again at the fifth chapter of Mark's Gospel about the healing of the woman with the issue of blood. Matthew, Mark, and Luke all record this same incident, but Mark goes into a little more detail about it and gives us more input than the other two Gospels.

MARK 5:25-34

25 And a certain woman, which had an issue of blood twelve years,

26 And had suffered many things of many physicians, and had spent all that she had, and was nothing bettered, but rather grew worse,

27 When she had heard of Jesus, came in the press behind, and touched his garment.

28 For she said, If I may touch but his clothes, I shall be whole.

29 And straightway the fountain of her blood was dried up; and she felt in her body that she was healed of that plague.

30 And Jesus, IMMEDIATELY knowing in himself that virtue [power] had gone out of him, turned him about in the press, and said, Who touched my clothes?

31 And his disciples said unto him, Thou seest the multitude thronging thee, and sayest thou, Who touched me?

32 And he looked round about to see her that had done this thing.

33 But the woman fearing and trembling, knowing what was done in her, came and fell down before him, and told him all the truth.

34 And he said unto her, Daughter, thy faith hath made thee whole; go in peace, and be whole of thy plague.

I want you to notice that Jesus immediately was aware that the anointing flowed *out from* Him. Also, notice that the woman with the issue of blood *cooperated with the anointing* that flowed from Jesus into her, and she was healed.

The healing anointing flowed out of Jesus' clothes and into the woman with the issue of blood. But Jesus said to her, *"Thy faith* hath made thee whole."* It wasn't the healing anointing alone that healed this woman. It was *her faith* in the healing anointing that healed her. Or we could say it like this: It was her faith *and* the healing anointing that healed her!

The healing power of God — the anointing — is a tangible substance. It is a heavenly materiality. Believe that, and it can begin to work for you.

Memory Text:
"And he [Jesus] *said unto her, Daughter, thy faith hath made thee whole; go in peace, and be whole of thy plague"*
(Mark 5:34)

Faith and Power — Two Ingredients for Receiving Healing, Part 2

Bible Texts: Acts 10:38; Mark 5:25-34; James 5:14-16

Central Truth: Even though the power is in manifestation, faith has to be exercised. For it's by faith that we receive any and every thing that comes from God.

We know that a person can receive divine healing any number of ways. We've talked about simply receiving healing by faith in the Word without any transfer of power, and we've talked about receiving through the healing anointing.

But notice something in the case of the woman with the issue of blood who was healed through the healing anointing. It wasn't the healing anointing alone that healed her. Something else was working with the anointing to bring about the healing. What was that something else? It was *faith*.

Jesus said to the woman, "Thy faith hath made thee whole." Some might say, "I thought it was the power which flowed out of Him that made her whole."

Well, really, it was a combination of the two. Both of them — faith and power — are important in their place. Someone who is anointed might minister the power of God, and the anointing may flow through him or her just as electricity flows through a conduit. Yet, although electricity is present all the time, unless someone turns a switch on, there's not going to be any *manifestation* of it.

In the same way, you have to turn the switch of faith on to receive a manifestation of the healing power of God!

Many people have thought that if the power of God was present, it would just manifest itself, regardless of whether or not anyone believed *in* it or believed *for* it. Then if there was no manifestation, they've thought,

Well, the power is not here. They'd start singing, "Oh, Lord, send the power just now."

Because they couldn't see the anointing or feel it in manifestation, they thought it wasn't there. But the power of God is always present everywhere. God didn't leave most of His power over in one state and then leave only a little bit of it wherever you are! No, wherever God is, *all* of His ability, *all* of His power, *all* of His capabilities are present.

Mixing Faith With the Power

So you can see that it's not a matter of the power getting the job done by itself. No, a person must appropriate or activate the power for himself for it to work for him. Certainly, it's true that it's ". . . *Not by might, nor by power, but by my spirit, saith the Lord . . .*" (Zech. 4:6), but we still have to cooperate with God's Spirit by believing in Him if we want to get the blessing. We've got to learn to mix faith with the power.

Now I tell this story sometimes, and it will further illustrate what I am talking about. In one church I pastored years ago, there was a woman, Sister _____, who had rheumatoid arthritis and was in a wheelchair. Her body had become as stiff as a board. You could take her out of the wheelchair, but you had to hold her and stand her up. She still looked like she was sitting down because her body was frozen in that stationary position.

We had a little prayer group that met every Wednesday afternoon at the church and prayed, and while we were praying one day, I said to the group, "Let's go down to Sister _____'s house and pray for her."

Everyone agreed, so I walked down to Sister _____'s house with my wife and the seven other ladies in the group. We knocked on the door, and Sister _____ invited us in. We talked a little bit, and I said, "Let's pray." I told the ladies to keep their eyes open because I expected Sister _____ to be healed, and I wanted everyone to see it.

Now, as I said earlier, a person can be specially anointed to minister healing — he or she can pray and seek God and minister with that anointing. But, then, you could also, as we sometimes say, "pray the power down." And that's what we did at Sister _____'s house — we prayed until the anointing came into manifestation. Then I pointed to her and said, "Now, my sister, arise and walk in the Name of Jesus!"

The power of God came, and all those ladies, including my wife, are witnesses that Sister _____ rose up out of the chair until she was hovering about two feet above it! And then that same Holy Ghost power brought her forward and she was just suspended in the air.

The Spirit *Upon*

Now if one is anointed with the Spirit, the anointing would flow *through* him, as we saw in Mark chapter 5. The anointing flowed through Jesus to the woman with the issue of blood. But in Sister _____'s case, this anointing came down, as it were, as a result of our *praying*. It came *upon* us.

Sister _____ looked around and saw that she was up above that wheelchair, and she began to whine and cry. She reached back and got hold of the arms of the chair and pulled it up under her. Then she fell back down in it.

Speaking by the Spirit of God, I said, "Sister, you don't have an ounce of faith, do you?" (Of course, I knew she had faith because she was a Spirit-filled Christian. What I was really saying was, "You don't have an ounce of faith when it comes to being healed of rheumatoid arthritis.")

She answered, "No, Brother Hagin, I'll go to my grave from this chair." And, I'm sad to say that she did.

But the power of God was there! It was that power which lifted her up. Now if she had responded to that — if she would have believed it and

accepted it — it would have healed her. That's the reason Jesus said in Mark chapter 5, "Daughter, *thy faith* hath made you whole."

The power was there at Sister _____'s house. It didn't come out of me. The anointing was in the room. We were all anointed with the Spirit as we "prayed it down," so to speak.

Prayer Avails Much

The easiest explanation for "praying the power down" comes by reading James 5:16. But let's start with verses 14 and 15.

JAMES 5:14-16
14 Is any sick among you? let him call for the elders of the church; and let them pray over him, anointing him with oil in the name of the Lord:
15 And the prayer of faith shall save the sick, and the Lord shall raise him up; and if he have committed sins, they shall be forgiven him.
16 Confess your faults one to another, and pray one for another, that ye may be healed. The effectual fervent prayer of a righteous man [does a little good. No!] **AVAILETH MUCH.**

The *King James Version* says, "availeth much," but *how* much? I like *The Amplified Bible*, because it tells us how much. It says, "... The earnest (heartfelt, continued) prayer of a righteous man makes tremendous

41

power available [dynamic in its working]."

Now notice that the prayer of a righteous man makes *tremendous power* available. This tremendous power is in the spirit realm all the time, isn't it? But the prayer of the righteous makes it *available*. Or, let's say it another way. The prayer of the righteous brings it into *manifestation*.

James says to pray one for another! That means it was scriptural for us to go down and pray for Sister ____. *Pray one for another.* Why? That you may be healed. Then it must be the will of God to heal, or He wouldn't tell us to pray for it.

The fervent effectual prayer of a righteous man availeth much. It makes tremendous power available, dynamic in its action. I like that. Well, you see, we did just what the Scripture said. We went down to Sister ____'s house, and we all prayed. And the power of God came into manifestation.

What was that power that lifted her up out of the chair? What was that power that pulled her away from it so that she was sitting in front of it, suspended in the air? It was dynamic Holy Ghost power!

Healing Power Is Always Present

Now, you see, that power is always there. *Power* is always present everywhere, because *God* is always present everywhere. But just because the power is present doesn't mean it's in manifestation. However, we know from reading James that the effectual fervent prayer of a righteous man makes tremendous power available! Well, we made it available in Sister ____'s case, but that was as far as we could go. We made it available, but she didn't take hold of it.

I couldn't take hold of it for her — I would have if I could have. Jesus *Himself*, couldn't have taken hold of it for her — He would have if He could have. That's the reason He said to the woman with the issue of blood, "Daughter, *thy* faith hath made thee whole."

Even though the power is in manifestation, faith has to be exercised. For it's by faith that we receive any and everything that comes from God.

God moved in a spectacular supernatural way on Sister ____'s behalf. Why wasn't she healed then? What did Jesus say to the woman with the issue of blood? "Daughter, *thy* faith. . . ." Whose faith? *Jesus'* faith? *Peter's* faith? The *apostles'* faith? No! *"THY* faith." It was the *woman's* faith that gave action to God's power!

Remember, God's power is present everywhere! But the fervent effectual prayer of a righteous man makes that tremendous power *available*! That's what we in Pentecostal circles called "praying the power down." But another way to say it is "praying the power into manifestation."

Well, thank God for the Word. And thank God for every avenue of healing: for simple faith in the Word of God; for the laying on of hands by believers and by those specially anointed to minister to the sick; and for supernatural manifestations of the healing power of God. We know that each of these methods of healing is scriptural and that they all work mightily on our behalf — *when we mix faith with the power!*

Memory Text:
" . . . The earnest (heartfelt, continued) prayer of a righteous man makes tremendous power available [dynamic in its working]"
(James 5:16, *Amplified*)

Faith and Power — Two Ingredients for Receiving Healing, Part 3

Bible Texts: Acts 10:38; Acts 6:3-6,8; Acts 8:14-16

Central Truth: We have to understand the mixing of faith with the power so we can realize the blessings and benefits of the anointing.

In the previous lessons, we began to look at two vital ingredients for receiving healing: *faith* and *power*. I mentioned that there are a number of methods for receiving healing recorded in the Word of God, such as: simple faith; the laying on of hands by believers and by those specially anointed to minister to the sick; and supernatural manifestations of the healing power of God. But I also noted that all of them require *your faith* and *the power of God.*

Remember concerning the power, Acts 10:38 indicates that the terms "the anointing," "the Holy Ghost," and "power" are virtually synonymous. This means that we are able to use them interchangeably when discussing the subject of the healing anointing and the power of God.

Remember that a good analogy for understanding the anointing or the power of God was made by Rev. John G. Lake when he said, *"Electricity is God's power in the natural realm; Holy Ghost power is God's power in the spirit realm."* As I state previously, just as electricity is in existence in the natural world, the power of God is in existence in the spirit world.

And just as man had to learn how to "plug in" to electricity and make it work for him, we must learn how to "plug in" to the heavenly electricity — the healing power of God — for it to be manifested in our life.

In the natural, when you turn a light switch on, electricity flows right into the lighting fixtures and lights up the room. When you turn the switch off, the lights go out. So in the spiritual realm, the thing that turns on the heavenly power could be called *the switch of faith!*

We've got to learn how to mix *faith* with the *power!*

Let's look at Acts chapter 6, and you'll see that what I'm saying is proven by God's Word.

ACTS 6:3-6
3 Wherefore, brethren, look ye out among you seven men of honest report, full of the Holy Ghost and wisdom, whom we may appoint over this business.
4 But we will give ourselves continually to prayer, and to the ministry of the word.
5 And the saying pleased the whole multitude: and they chose Stephen, a man full of FAITH and of THE HOLY GHOST, and Philip, and Prochorus, and Nicanor, and Timon, and Parmenas, and Nicolas a proselyte of Antioch:
6 Whom they set before the apostles: and when they had prayed, they laid their hands on them.

Just to give you some background and history, here in Acts chapter 6 during the early days of the Church, the believers had "all things in common" (Acts 2:44). The disciples, the twelve apostles, were the only ministers the believers had at the beginning of the Early Church. It was a baby Church, just starting, and the

Church didn't exist anywhere else except in Jerusalem at that time.

You see, Jesus had said to go into all the world and preach the Gospel to every creature (Mark 16:15). He also said in Acts 1:8 that ". . . *after that the Holy Ghost is come upon you . . . ye shall be witnesses unto me both in Jerusalem, and in all Judaea, and in Samaria, and unto the uttermost part of the earth."* Yet the believers hadn't witnessed to anyone anywhere except in Jerusalem.

So there in Jerusalem, the believers had all things in common, but some of them felt as if they were being neglected in the daily ministrations. So the Twelve said, *"Wherefore, brethren, look ye out among you seven men of HONEST REPORT, FULL OF THE HOLY GHOST and WISDOM, whom we may appoint over this business"* (Acts 6:3).

The men they were looking for had to meet three requirements. They had to: 1) have an honest report; 2) be full of the Holy Ghost; and 3) be full of wisdom.

Full of Faith and Power

Verse 5 goes on to list the seven men who were chosen to oversee the daily ministrations. Now all seven of these men were full of the Holy Ghost. That was one of the qualifications — that they be full of the Holy Ghost. But it says about Stephen that he was full of faith *and* the Holy Ghost or power. And there were certain miracles and signs that followed Stephen's mix of faith and power.

ACTS 6:8

8 And Stephen, FULL OF FAITH AND POWER, did great wonders and miracles among the people.

You see, if you are full of the Holy Ghost, you're full of power. I mean, you've got the Powerhouse in you! Well, every one of those seven men were full of power. But that doesn't mean that every one of them was full of faith.

Did you ever stop to think about the fact that every Spirit-filled believer — every believer who maintains the Spirit-filled experience — is full of power. He doesn't have to *get* full; he *is* full.

Now to be filled with the Spirit is to be filled with power. Jesus said in Acts 1:8, *"But ye shall receive POWER, after that the HOLY GHOST is come upon you . . . ."*

So we read in Acts 6:3 that the apostles said, *". . . look ye out among you seven men of honest report, FULL OF THE HOLY GHOST* [power] *and wisdom, whom we may appoint over this business."*

All seven men listed in Acts 6:5 were full of the Holy Ghost. That means that all seven of these men were full of *power*. But apparently, there was only one of them who did any miracles and signs among the people, and that was Stephen.

Every one of them had the power to do the miracles and signs. Why didn't they do them then? *Because it takes faith to give action to the power!*

Faith Activates the Power

You can see where we as Spirit-filled believers and Pentecostal people, particularly in days gone by, have missed it. We've thought that if we had the power, the miracles and the wonders would just automatically follow.

But they won't. We saw that in Acts chapter 6. All seven of those men were full of power, but only one of them did any miracles or wonders, and that was Stephen. And Stephen wasn't even one of the Twelve. He wasn't a preacher or an apostle or an evangelist. In fact, according to the Scripture, he never did become an evangelist or an apostle or pastor; he lived and died a deacon.

ACTS 6:8

8 And Stephen, full of faith and power, did great wonders and miracles among the people.

Stephen didn't do great wonders and miracles just by being full of power. No, he was full of faith *and* power. And so we know that power by itself won't get the job done. You have to mix faith *with* the power to get the power to work.

Did you notice that the same thing is true in the case of an individual's healing? For example, in the case of the woman with the issue of blood, Jesus knew immediately that power had gone out of Him. But He didn't say, "Daughter, My *power* hath made thee whole." No, He said, "Daughter, thy *faith* hath made thee whole" (Mark 5:34). It was her faith mixed with the power that healed her.

Faith Comes by Hearing

Also, notice that when Jesus and His disciples crossed over the Sea of Galilee to the land of Gennesaret in Matthew chapter 14, the people of that place "had knowledge of Jesus" and brought the sick and diseased to Him. As the sick and the diseased touched the hem of Jesus' garment, they were made whole (vv. 35, 36).

But notice the men of Gennesaret did that *when* they "had knowledge of Him." They had to have heard about Jesus to have knowledge of Him. Well, we know that "faith comes by hearing, and hearing by the Word of God" (Rom. 10:17). So again, faith was involved.

Then in Luke chapter 6, it says the multitude came to hear Jesus and to be healed of their diseases. It said they sought to touch Jesus, for there went virtue or power out of Him and healed them all. But notice they came to *hear* and to be healed. They heard *first*, then faith came, and then they sought to touch Him.

People need to understand the healing anointing. They need to know that it exists, but just as importantly, they need to know how to get that anointing to work and produce results in their lives. They need to believe or have faith in the healing power of God.

Memory Text:
"And Stephen, full of faith and power, did great wonders and miracles among the people"
(Acts 6:8)

Faith and Power — Two Ingredients for Receiving Healing, Part 4

Bible Texts: Acts 10:44; Acts 8:14-16; Hebrews 4:2; Acts 19:11-12; Mark 11:22-24

Central Truth: The Holy Ghost is ever-present with all the power He has! You can mix your faith with the power that is present, whether the power is in manifestation or not, and receive your healing by faith.

Sometimes, the healing power of God is ministered to a sick person so that the person is manifestly supercharged with heavenly electricity. *Yet no real or final healing takes place until something occurs that releases the faith of the individual.*

After I started preaching, I would teach people faith. Once in a while, we'd have manifestations of the Spirit or the anointing, and folks would receive healing as a result of their faith mixed with the power of God. But I'd see a lot of people healed when we didn't feel anything. We just believed, and it happened!

Yet, right on the other hand, even back then, people I'd pray for would say sometimes, "Something's all over me!" Well, I knew they were talking about the same thing that happened to me when I was healed. And those

people were healed, because He was present! That same Spirit was present, and they mixed faith with the power and were healed!

Manifested Power

Now I want to show you something about mixing faith with the power to receive healing. When I was young and the new pastor of a Full Gospel church in northcentral Texas, we had just moved into the parsonage and were unloading boxes and straightening things up.

There was a knock on the parsonage door. I went to the door and there stood a little cotton-headed boy. Now someone asked me, "What do you mean, 'cotton-headed'?" Well, I just mean his hair was white like cotton. He was about nine years old. He said, "Momma wants you to come and pray for her."

I said, "Who's momma?" because I didn't know him — I had only been the pastor for two Sundays. I hadn't gotten acquainted with everyone yet.

The little boy told me his momma's name, and I recognized her as being one of the Sunday school teachers. So I said, "Son, stand right there. I'll put on my tie and coat, and you can show me the way to go because I don't know where you live."

I took the little bottle of anointing oil that I had, and we went to the little boy's house. I anointed this boy's momma with oil, laid hands on her, prayed, and got up to leave.

She said, "Brother B____ [and she gave the name of the former pastor] always prayed till the power fell."

I knew that the power of God does "fall" because the Bible said that while Peter yet spake unto them, the Holy Ghost fell on them (Acts 10:44). And Acts 8 also refers to the Holy Ghost this way.

ACTS 8:14-16
14 Now when the apostles which were at Jerusalem heard that Samaria had received the word of God, they sent unto them Peter and John:
15 Who, when they were come down, prayed for them, that they might receive the Holy Ghost:

16 (For as yet he was FALLEN UPON none of them. . . .)

That's the part I want you to get. The Holy Ghost *does* fall on people — like rain. In fact, latter rain is a type of the Holy Ghost.

'Praying the Power Down'

Back in 1939, I didn't know exactly what to do when she said "pray the power down" because I was new in Pentecostal circles. I didn't know how they did things. But I figured if that was the way the former pastor did it, then that was the way to do it. So I got back down on my knees and prayed till the power fell. It took me an hour and a half, but I prayed the power down! The house shook, the bed shook, and the woman shook.

It was summertime — the sky was blue with just a few white clouds. There wasn't a leaf stirring on any tree. And yet the windows rattled! Well, I got up off my knees and went home to the parsonage.

That afternoon there was a knock on the parsonage door. I went to the door and there stood that little cotton-headed boy. He said, "Momma wants you to come and pray for her."

I said, "I thought she got healed this morning."

He said, "She did, but she's worse now."

So I went down there and prayed the power down again — the power fell, she shook, the bed shook, the house shook, and the windows shook. So I went back to the parsonage.

The next day there was another knock on the door. I went to the door, and there stood that little cotton-headed boy. He said, "Momma wants you to come and pray for her."

I said, "I thought she got healed twice yesterday."

"Well, she did, but she's hurting worse today."

So I went down there again and prayed the power down. By that time, I was becoming an expert at praying the power down, so it didn't take an hour and a half to pray it down. I did it in an hour, and then I went home.

The next day there was a knock on the door, so I went to the door, and there stood that cotton-headed boy! The same scenario happened again and again until I finally got to where I could pray the power down in thirty minutes. She shook, the bed shook, the windows rattled, and the house shook. And that went on, and on, and on.

If you think I'm exaggerating, we'll skip ahead to three years later. This went on for three years! We had been building onto the parsonage,

and there was a little work left to finish. I worked a little late on it one night because I didn't want to have to work the next day. After I finished, I was getting ready for church because we were having revival that night. As I was quickly getting ready, I heard my wife let someone in the house. I looked up, and there was that cotton-headed boy.

Now he and I had been working together so long that we knew what the other was thinking. So I said, before he could say it, "Yeah, I know, momma wants me to come and pray for her."

When the cotton-headed boy arrived, it was only about ten minutes until the church service was supposed to start. (The parsonage was right next door, so I still had plenty of time to get to the church.)

I was about to say, "Will it be all right to come after church?" I had just started to speak when he said, "No, she said to come before church. She's hurting awfully bad!"

I wondered how in the world I was going to get down there and pray the power down and get back and start church in ten minutes. I quickly put my tie and coat on.

I had a car, but I knew I could get there faster by going down the back alley. So I ran out of the parsonage, ran behind the church, down one alley, back up another alley, across the street, down another alley, and knocked on the door.

She told me to come in. I had my bottle of oil out before I even got in the door. I went in and anointed her with oil. I said, "Oh, God, heal this woman in the Name of Jesus. You said if we'd ask in Your Name, You'd do it, so You've done it. Amen." That's exactly what I said, and I said it double time!

I put the top on my bottle of oil and headed for the door — I had to go back and start church! She started to say something, but I said, "I know, Sister, you're hurting worse now than you did when I came in here a few seconds ago. But you're healed, and the next time I see you, you'll tell me it's so." And I ran out and slammed the door.

I ran up one alley, across the street, up another alley, behind the church, and went in through a side door. I looked at my watch — it was exactly time to start. We started church, sang, took up an offering for the evangelist, and made the announcements.

Just before the evangelist was going to speak, I said, "Let's have about three testimonies, one from each section. Someone who has been saved, healed, or baptized with the Holy Ghost during this revival, stand up and give your testimony."

So one person stood and testified. Then another one from a different section stood and testified. About that time, the double doors in the back of the church opened. And this lady, Sister S____, who'd been having me pray the power down for *three years*, came in. I guess she thought we were having a testimony meeting, because she came down the aisle waving her arms and said, "It's just like you said, Brother Hagin. You hadn't been gone ten minutes when every pain and every symptom left me."

Hallelujah! I pastored that woman nearly eighteen more months and never did have to go pray for her again!

Keeping Your Healing

Thank God for the power. But remember this, if you don't believe God — the power can shake the house and everything else, and *still* nothing will happen to *you*. This lady received her healing and finally *kept* it because she believed God herself.

The reason I tell this story is to show that although the healing power may be ministered to a person, and though that person may manifestly be supercharged with the power of God, no real and final healing will take place until something occurs that releases the faith of the individual.

The Bible says in Hebrews 4:2, *"For unto us was the gospel preached, as well as unto them* [talking about Israel]: *but the word preached did not profit them, NOT BEING MIXED WITH FAITH in them that heard it."*

One way to receive the healing power, of course, is through the laying on of hands (Mark 16:18). Or you could receive it from a cloth or a handkerchief that has absorbed the anointing (Acts 19:11-12). On the other hand, receiving healing that way is only *one* way to receive. Remember I said you could receive healing by acting in simple faith on the Word of God, as I did to receive my healing (Mark 11:22-24).

The Holy Ghost is ever-present with all the power He has! You can mix your faith with the power that is present, whether the power is in manifestation or not, and receive your healing by faith.

In conclusion, let's sum up a few things about the healing power of God. When we understand some things about the anointing, we can appropriate it for ourselves and reap the benefit of this power in our own lives.

The healing anointing is a tangible substance. And the Word of God *reveals to us* the rules and laws that govern its operation.

The Lord Jesus Christ revealed and applied the laws of the Spirit, which demonstrated the fact that the healing power of God is a tangible substance, a heavenly materiality.

Now you'll not receive any of this power from Heaven if you don't believe there's any there. If you don't believe it exists, you'll never get it applied to your circumstances so that it will do you any good. The healing power of God will not benefit you until you believe in it, lay hold of it intelligently by faith, and simply receive it.

But, thank God, through your faith in the holy written Word and in the mighty power of God, you *can* receive divine healing! By believing what God's Word says about the healing anointing, you can enjoy all the blessings and benefits of this power from Heaven that is available to us today.

✳
Memory Text:
"For unto us was the gospel preached, as well as unto them: but the word preached did not profit them, NOT BEING MIXED WITH FAITH in them that heard it"
(Heb. 4:2)

The Gifts of the Spirit

Bible Texts: 1 Corinthians 12:1,7-11; Ephesians 2:8; Galatians 5:22; Daniel 6:1-23

Central Truth: The gift of faith is a gift of the Spirit to the believer that he might receive a miracle.

We are discussing biblical ways to receive healing. There are many different methods listed in the Bible whereby you can receive healing. One way to receive healing is through the manifestation of one of the gifts of the Spirit.

The nine gifts of the Spirit listed in First Corinthians 12:8-10 are often divided into three separate categories, because they naturally seem to fit there. Any one of the nine gifts may be used, as the Spirit wills, to aid in the area of healing. The most common spiritual gifts used concerning healing are the power gifts: the working of miracles, the gift of faith, and the gifts of healing. And these "power" gifts will very often work together.

Working of miracles is defined as a divine intervention in the ordinary course of nature that can't be explained in the natural. For example, the dividing of a stream by the sweep of a mantle is an example of the working of miracles in operation (2 Kings 2:14). After Elijah ascended into Heaven in a chariot in the whirlwind, Elisha received his mantle and smote the Jordan River. Dividing the waters by a sweep of his mantle was the working of miracles because that was a supernatural intervention in the ordinary course of nature.

In the area of healing, many times miracles are received. However this is not necessarily the working of miracles but is simply called healing miracles. Everything that God does is miraculous, in a sense, but receiving healing by supernatural means is not a miracle in the same sense that turning common dust into insects just by a gesture is a miracle (Exod. 8:16), or turning common water into wine just by speaking a word is a miracle (John 2:7-11). Those two occurrences are examples of the working of miracles.

Although in the Old Testament people were healed and the gifts of healings were in operation, gifts of healings were more commonly in operation in the New Testament than they were in the Old Testament.

On the other hand, the working of miracles was more prominent or more commonly manifested in the Old Testament than in the New Testament, with the exception of the gift of working of miracles in Jesus' ministry.

The Gift of Faith

Now I want to focus on the gift of faith. I like the *Weymouth* translation of First Corinthians 12:9, because it calls this spiritual gift "special faith." You see, this faith is *special* faith because every believer already has faith (Rom. 12:3).

For example, there is *saving* faith, or faith to receive salvation, which is also a gift of God.

EPHESIANS 2:8
8 For by grace are ye SAVED THROUGH FAITH; and that not of yourselves: it is the gift of God.

The faith by which you are saved is a gift of God, but it is given to you through hearing the Word. The Bible says, *"So then faith* [saving faith] *cometh by hearing, and hearing by the WORD OF GOD"* (Rom. 10:17). But the gift of faith is distinct from saving faith. It is a supernatural manifestation of one of the nine gifts of the Spirit.

The gift of faith is a gift of the Spirit to the believer that he might *receive* a miracle, whereas the working of miracles is a gift of the Spirit to the believer that he might *work* a miracle. (One gift *receives* something, and the other *does* something.) But these gifts are very closely related. We're just differentiating between them for the purpose of defining them.

So then, we said that the *gift of faith* is separate and distinct from *saving faith*. It is also distinct from the *fruit* of faith that we're taught about in the New Testament.

GALATIANS 5:22
22 . . . the fruit of the Spirit is love, joy, peace, longsuffering, gentleness, goodness, FAITH.

Galatians 5:22 says that faith is a fruit of the Spirit. However, if you look up this word in the original Greek translation, you will find that it refers to *faithfulness*.

The fruit of the Spirit are for *character*, but the gifts of the Spirit are for *power*. A fruit is something that grows. So faith, or faithfulness, is a spiritual fruit that grows in the life of the Christian to establish him in spiritual character. The *gift of faith*, however, is given supernaturally by the Spirit of God, as He wills (1 Cor. 12:11).

So you can see that there are different kinds of faith. Saving faith comes before salvation, and the fruit of faith comes or develops after salvation. But the manifestation of the gift of faith comes after the baptism in the Holy Spirit, as the Spirit wills.

Many times people — even Christians — who haven't studied the Bible say, "Well, if God gives me faith, I'll have it. And if He doesn't, I won't." They read in First Corinthians 12:9, "to another is given faith," and they may think that's how all faith works. But that verse is talking about the gift of faith, which is separate from all other kinds of faith. The gift of faith is a gift of the Spirit to the believer that he might receive a miracle!

Remember, the working of miracles employs faith that actively *works* a miracle. But the gift of faith employs faith that passively *expects* a miracle as a sustained or continuous action. There may not be anything that the person sees at the

moment to confirm that he has his answer. But special faith will carry over a long period of time. In other words, its manifestation can be sustained or continued for the purpose of receiving a miracle.

A Supernatural Endowment

The gift of faith is also a supernatural endowment by the Holy Spirit whereby that which is uttered or desired by man, or spoken by God, eventually comes to pass. In other words, when this power gift is in operation, you believe God in such a way that God honors your word as His own and miraculously brings to pass whatever you believe or say. So the miracle, utterance, assurance, curse or blessing, creation or destruction, or removal or alteration has to manifest when it has been spoken under the inspiration of this gift.

In my own life, I've always been one to believe God's Word and act upon it. But I'm conscious of times when special faith is operating in my life. And it doesn't bother me a bit in the world whether or not I see anything. I'll just laugh right in the face of the circumstances, because I know that the Word has been spoken and it shall to come to pass!

Faith To Raise the Dead

Smith Wigglesworth said that if you will take a step of faith — use the measure of faith you have as a Christian — when you come to the end of that faith, very often this supernatural gift of special faith will take over.

Under Wigglesworth's ministry, at least three different people were raised from the dead. In his book *Ever Increasing Faith*, Wigglesworth related one instance of his neighbor being raised from the dead. [1]

One day Wigglesworth visited a sick neighbor who had been close to death. After coming home from an open-air meeting the following day, Wigglesworth learned that his wife Polly was at this neighbor's house. As Wigglesworth approached the house, he heard screaming. He went inside and found the sick man's wife, crying, "He's gone! He's gone!"

Wigglesworth said, "I just passed by the man's wife and went into the room. Immediately, I saw that he was gone. I could not understand it, but I began to pray. My wife was always afraid that I would go too far, and she laid hold of me and said, 'Don't, Dad! Don't you see that he is dead?' But I continued praying.

"I got as far as I could with my own faith, and then God laid hold of me. It was such a laying hold that I could believe for anything. The faith of the Lord Jesus laid hold of me, and a solid peace came into my heart. I shouted, 'He lives! He lives! He lives!'

And my neighbor is still living today."

Well, you know as well as I do, that receiving the dead back to life is beyond anyone's ordinary faith. In our ordinary faith, we could pull a dead person off his deathbed, stand him up, and tell him to walk. But that doesn't mean he would begin to walk. Why not? Because it would take a miracle — and it takes a supernatural manifestation of God's power to receive a miracle from God!

As I said before, the working of miracles *performs* a miracle, but the gift of faith *receives* a miracle. So the working of miracles is more of an *act*, whereas the gift of faith is more of a *process*.

We can see that by the gift of faith, the miraculous was manifested in the Scriptures. People were supernaturally fed and sustained. Angels stood guard over and protected the servants of God. Men were delivered from the ferocity of beasts. And the dead were raised to life. But the *present-day* use of this power gift is still the same.

In the same way that the gift of faith was manifested in Bible days, it can be manifested to receive supernatural blessings, protection, or sustenance today. By this power gift, evil spirits can be cast out and the dead can be raised. But it takes supernatural faith — special faith — for those things to happen!

The Gifts Work Together

As I have mentioned, the three power gifts — the working of miracles, the gift of faith, and the gifts of healings — will very often work together. In the case of raising the dead, all three of these power gifts operate together.

First of all, in raising the dead, it takes supernatural faith — the gift of special faith — to call a person's spirit back after it has left the body. Then it takes the working of miracles because the body would have started to deteriorate, as in the case of Lazarus (John 11:39).

And then raising the dead also takes the gifts of healings because if the person who was raised from the dead wasn't healed, whatever he died from would still affect his body and he would die again. So the person would have to be healed too. Therefore, all three of the power gifts are in manifestation when someone is raised from the dead.

Gifts of Healings

We have looked at the "power" gifts of the Spirit — the gifts that *do* something — mentioned in First Corinthians 12:9 and 10. We have discussed the *working of miracles*

and the *gift of faith*. Now I want to focus on the *gifts of healings*.

In the original Greek translation of First Corinthians 12:9 and 30, this gift is listed as "gifts of healings" — both *gifts* and *healings* are plural. Therefore, we will refer to this spiritual gift as the *gifts of healings*.

As we study the gifts of healings in Scripture, we see that they are manifested for the supernatural healing of diseases and infirmities without natural means of any sort.

For example, Luke, the writer of the Acts of the Apostles and the Gospel that bears his name, was a medical doctor by profession. He accompanied Paul on many missionary journeys and was traveling with him when they were shipwrecked on the island of Melita. When we read the account in Acts 28, nothing is ever said about Luke ministering to anyone while they were there. But the Bible says that Paul ministered to several on the island who were sick or had diseases, and they were healed. How? By the supernatural power of God!

ACTS 28:8,9
8 And it came to pass, that the father of Publius lay sick of a fever and of a bloody flux: to whom PAUL ENTERED IN, AND PRAYED, AND LAID HIS HANDS ON HIM, AND HEALED HIM.

9 So when this was done, OTHERS ALSO, WHICH HAD DISEASES IN THE ISLAND, CAME, AND WERE HEALED.

Now some have mistakenly thought that the gifts of healings refer to the fact that God has given us doctors and medical science. Of course, we believe in medical science and doctors, and thank God for what they can do — we are certainly not opposed to them. But the gifts of the Spirit are *supernatural*. They have nothing to do with medical science.

Healing that is supernatural doesn't come by a diagnosis and the prescribing of treatment. It comes by the laying on of hands, anointing with oil, or sometimes just speaking God's Word in faith! So we not only believe in *natural* healing, but we also believe in *supernatural* healing!

---

[1]Smith Wigglesworth, *Ever Increasing Faith*, (Springfield, Missouri: Gospel Publishing House, 1971), pp. 138,139.

✳
Memory Text:
"But the manifestation of the Spirit is given to every man to profit withal"
(1 Cor. 12:7)

The Gifts of the Spirit, Part 2

Bible Texts: 1 Corinthians 12:7-9,28-30; Acts 28:8,9; Luke 4:18; Acts 10:38; Acts 3:2-6

Central Truth: When the gifts of healings are in operation, they're manifested through another person unto you, as the Spirit wills.

The Bible is full of examples of the gifts of healings in operation — delivering the sick and destroying the works of the devil in a person's human body — especially through Jesus' ministry. However, I often point out the fact that Jesus ministered as a prophet anointed by the Holy Ghost.

Notice, for instance, what Jesus said of Himself in the synagogue, reading from the Prophet Isaiah: *"The Spirit of the Lord is upon me, because HE HATH ANOINTED ME . . ."* (Luke 4:18). Then in Acts 10:38, Peter said, *". . .GOD ANOINTED JESUS of Nazareth with the Holy Ghost and with power: who went about doing good, and healing all . . . ."*

Jesus never healed anyone until *after* He was anointed with the Holy Ghost and power. And yet He was just as much the Son of God when He was twenty-five years old as He was at age thirty. So Jesus didn't heal the sick by some power that was inherent in Him as the Second Person of the Trinity. He healed them the same way anyone else would minister to the sick today — by the anointing of the Spirit or the manifestation of the gifts of healings!

Now the main thing we need to understand is that there is a difference between the manifestation of the gifts of healings and receiving healing by one's own faith in God's Word.

When I teach, I emphasize that people can receive healing simply by exercising faith in the Word of God — because it always works. Many of you know my testimony of how I received healing as a young Baptist boy reading Grandma's Methodist Bible. I wasn't healed because I believed in divine healing, necessarily. I was healed by *acting* and *standing* on Mark 11:24!

I read in Mark 11:24 that Jesus said, ". . .*What things soever ye DESIRE, when ye pray, believe that ye receive them, and ye shall have them.*" Well, I desired healing. So I prayed and began to say: "I believe I receive healing for my deformed heart, I believe I receive healing for my paralyzed body, I believe I receive healing for my incurable blood condition," and so forth.

To make a long story short, God's healing power was manifested in my body. No one laid hands on me. That power came unto me directly from God. But when the *gifts of healings* are in operation, they're manifested *through another person* unto you, as the Spirit wills. That's the difference. The healing always comes from God, however.

Healing as a Gift vs. Gifts of Healings

Now some have said, "Any time you receive healing, it's a manifestation of the gifts of healings." But I disagree with that statement. Healing is a gift, all right, in the general sense that anything you receive from God would be a gift. But that doesn't necessarily mean that these spiri-tual gifts are in operation. For example, that wasn't the case when I received healing as a young boy on the bed of sickness.

Others have taken this reasoning one step further, saying, "Healing is a gift. So any time you get healed, *you* have received a gift of healing." But I can't accept that explanation either, because it doesn't line up with Scripture. Take a look at First Corinthians 12:28-30.

1 CORINTHIANS 12:28-30
28 And GOD HATH SET SOME IN THE CHURCH, first apostles, secondarily prophets, thirdly teachers, after that miracles, THEN GIFTS OF HEALINGS, helps, governments, diversities of tongues.
29 Are all apostles? are all prophets? are all teachers? are all workers of miracles?
30 HAVE ALL THE GIFTS OF HEALING [healings]? . . .

Notice in verse 28 that God set "some" in the Church. Paul isn't talking about spiritual gifts, because he said in verse 27, *"Now ye are the body of Christ, and MEMBERS in particular."* No, Paul is referring to men equipped with spiritual gifts. God set *members equipped with spiritual gifts* in the Church — first, apostles; secondarily, prophets; thirdly, teachers; and so forth.

You see, the "gift" of the apostle, prophet, or teacher is a ministry gift given to the Church, not an individual gift that someone might receive (Eph. 4:8,11). In other words, it's not given to bless *you*! It's given in order to bless *others*. It's a ministry!

First Corinthians 12:28 goes on to say, "*after that* miracles," meaning: "*After those who are equipped with the ministry gifts which Paul just mentioned*, there are some in the ministry who are equipped with the gift of the working of miracles." (A better way to say it would be that the gift of the working of miracles operates by the Spirit more consistently in some people's ministries.)

Next Paul mentions the gifts of healings, and he asks a few rhetorical questions: "Does everyone have the ministry of an apostle?" Certainly not. "Does everyone have the ministry of a prophet?" No. "Does everyone have the ministry of the teacher?" No. We could all teach to some extent, of course. But there are those whom God has put in the Church who are specifically equipped or anointed by the Holy Spirit with a teaching gift.

So, you see, the gifts of healings are not referring to gifts given to individuals to bless them personally. They are *ministries* of healing that are given to some in order to bless others. I like to say it this way: The gifts of healings are supernatural manifestations of the Spirit that are manifested *through someone* to *someone else*!

Laying On of Hands

When I started out in the healing ministry as a Baptist boy preacher, I wasn't conscious of any kind of anointing or special manifestation of the Spirit. I just prayed for people in faith through the laying on of hands and anointing with oil. I received the baptism of the Holy Ghost later, but I continued to pray for the sick the same way.

Then in 1938, I accepted the pastorate of a little Full Gospel church in the blacklands of north-central Texas, where I met my wife Oretha. After we were married, Oretha and I lived with her folks, who owned a large farmhouse. Neither she nor her parents had received the baptism of the Holy Ghost yet, so when we all gathered to pray, I did my best to behave myself.

But one night we got to praying and I unconsciously started praying in tongues right out loud. I prayed in tongues approximately 45 minutes, and then the Spirit of God said to me, "Lay your hand on your wife, and I'll fill her with the Holy Ghost." So I reached out my hand and laid it on top of Oretha's head.

Oretha had never sought the Holy Ghost a minute in her life, but the second I laid my hand on her head, she threw up both hands and started talking in tongues instantly. She never stammered or stuttered. She just began speaking fluently in other tongues as the Spirit of the Lord gave her utterance.

Special Anointing

Well, that same night around midnight, the Lord ministered to me by His Spirit concerning the gifts of healings and His sending me out to minister to the sick. Now as I said, I would anoint people with oil and lay hands on them for healing, simply praying with them in faith. In other words, none of the gifts of the Spirit were in operation. God's healing power would manifest itself directly unto *them*.

But on occasion I would be conscious of a manifestation of God's power working through *me*. That didn't always happen (it was as the Spirit willed), but I was aware of it when it did. I really didn't do a whole lot about it, though, except yield to the Spirit of God.

Ten years later I was pastoring a church in east Texas, and I started to become dissatisfied spiritually. Naturally speaking, I had every cause in the world to feel good and rejoice. Folks had been getting saved, filled

with the Spirit, and healed in the church. But I was just flat *dissatisfied*.

So I spent some concentrated time shut up in the church, praying, reading my Bible, and seeking God about ministry. While I was at the altar praying one day, the Lord asked me: "What are you going to do about the healing ministry and what I said to you ten years ago in that little farmhouse in north-central Texas?"

I said, "To tell You the truth, Lord, I didn't intend to do anything about it."

He said, "You're going to have to — or else."

Well, I had run into some of the Lord's "or else's" through the years, so I said to Him, "Yes, Sir! I believe I will." And I left the last church I pastored in February 1949 to go out into field ministry and endeavor to do what God had called me to do.

Heart Trouble

One night while holding a meeting in a Full Gospel church in Henderson, Texas, I was praying for the sick by the laying on of hands. A woman from the church came up, and the Spirit of God gave me a word of knowledge concerning her: "Thy heart is not right with God."

I knew I should have spoken that word out, but I was reluctant. (That's a terrible thing to have to tell someone.) So I bit my tongue and shut my mouth to keep from saying anything. And, suddenly, the anointing lifted from me like a cloud and floated away.

I had been staying in the parsonage as the pastor's guest, and the minute I lay down to go to sleep that night, it felt as if my heart just stopped. I reached up to feel my chest and couldn't feel any heartbeat, just a faint fluttering or shaking. I rolled out of bed and hit the cold linoleum floor, yelling at the top of my voice: "Lord, I'll obey You next time! I'll do what You want me to do!" I was so loud that I woke the pastor and his wife in their bedroom at the opposite end of the house!

I made my way to the dining room and called out to the pastor to come pray for me. As death fastened its final throes on me, I could feel myself slipping out of my body. I'd had the same experience twice before, so I knew that death had come.

I wanted to leave a word for the pastor to tell my wife and children. But when I opened my mouth to speak, I began to prophesy instead. I had never done much prophesying before, but I started to prophesy out

of my spirit — and God began to speak to me through my own words.

You see, I had not fully obeyed Him in some areas concerning the gifts of the Spirit, because I was afraid what people would think. I thought they'd think I was trying to attract attention to myself if I ministered the way He was leading me when His gifts were in manifestation.

But the Spirit of the Lord said to me: "When Peter and John saw the man who was crippled at the gate called Beautiful, Peter stopped and said to him, 'Look on us!'" (Acts 3:4).

ACTS 3:2-6
2 And a certain man lame from his mother's womb was carried, whom they laid daily at the gate of the temple which is called Beautiful....
3 Who seeing Peter and John about to go into the temple asked an alms.
4 And Peter, fastening his eyes upon him with John, said, LOOK ON US.
5 And he gave heed unto them, EXPECTING TO RECEIVE SOMETHING OF THEM.
6 Then Peter said, Silver and gold have I none; but such as I have give I thee: In the name of Jesus Christ of Nazareth rise up and walk.

Expectancy

As I continued to speak out of my spirit, the Lord explained: "Peter didn't say that to draw attention to John and himself or to brag about something they had. He said it in order to raise the man's expectancy — so that he would expect to receive what Peter and John had from God" (v. 5)!

Then the Spirit of the Lord said to me, "It wouldn't have done any good for Peter to say, 'The gifts of healings are in operation,' because the man wouldn't have known anything about that. The New Testament had not yet been written.

"You see, people can be healed directly from Me because they believe and exercise faith in the promises of God, just as you did. But many people are not at the place spiritually where they can receive healing on their own. Therefore, I want you to tell them that I have anointed you and sent you to minister to the sick.

"When you do that, you're not attracting attention to yourself, you're arousing the people's expectancy. If you can just arouse their expectancy, they wouldn't need any more faith than just to expect Me to heal them *through* you as My gifts are in manifestation."

I saw the difference then. And that's what I want to get over to you. *You can be healed directly, simply by believing God — and I believe that's the best way to receive healing.* But everyone is not going to receive that way. That's why we need to pray along these lines.

Pray what? That all would have the gifts of healings? No, we already saw in First Corinthians chapter 12 that everyone will not have the gifts of healings operating through them. But thank God, *some will!*

Well, thank God for the privilege to believe and act on God's Word. We should be doing that continually. But we can also pray that the gifts of healings would be supernaturally manifested among us even more, and expect God's power to flow unto others *through* members of His Body, as the Spirit wills!

✳
Memory Text:
"And Peter, fastening his eyes upon him with John, said, Look on us. And he gave heed unto them, expecting to receive something of them"
(Acts 3:4,5)

The Healing Anointing

Bible Texts: Mark 16:18; Acts 10:38; John 3:34;
Matthew 14:35,36; Mark 5:27; Acts 19:11,12

Central Truth: The laying on of hands is a point
of contact that releases the healing power of God.

In previous lessons, we discussed how faith will activate the healing power of God. You can activate the healing power by your own faith in the Word of God, as I did on the eighth day of August, 1934. By faith, I "plugged in" to the healing power of God that was present in my room, and was raised up from the bed of sickness.

We have also discussed how you can receive healing by the laying on of hands. We know this method is scriptural because we are told in Mark's Gospel to lay hands on the sick (Mark 16:18). Any believer can lay hands on the sick based on this particular verse of Scripture. But there are also those who are specially anointed to minster healing to the sick.

In this lesson, I want to further discuss the healing anointing, with a focus on the ways the anointing may be transferred by a person specially anointed to minister healing.

As I said in a previous lesson, Acts 10:38 indicates that the terms, "the anointing," "the Holy Ghost," and "power" are virtually synonymous. This means that we are able to use these terms interchangeably when discussing the subject of the healing anointing and the power of God.

Concerning the individual anointing, we know that God anoints individuals to minister. There are different offices in which God calls them to minister — the office of the apostle, prophet, evangelist, pastor, and teacher. Jesus stood in all five of

67

them, so He had the anointing that goes with every office.

Jesus had the anointing *without measure* (John 3:34). Members of the Body of Christ have the anointing *in a measure*.

Of course, Jesus was and is the Son of God. But Jesus was not *ministering* as the Son of God. He was *ministering* as a mere man anointed with the Holy Ghost! If Jesus was ministering on the earth as the Son of God and not as a man, then He wouldn't need to be anointed. But the Bible plainly says Jesus was anointed to minister on the earth (Luke 4:18; Acts 10:38).

Characteristics of the Healing Anointing

I want to look at some characteristics of the anointing, which will help you understand the way it works. First, the anointing is *transmittable*.

MATTHEW 14:35,36
35 And when the men of that place had knowledge of him [Jesus], they sent out into all that country round about, and brought unto him all that were diseased;
36 And besought him that they might only touch the HEM of his garment: and as many as touched were made perfectly whole.

You'll notice that in Matthew chapter 14, those people sought to touch the hem of Jesus' garment. They didn't touch *Him*; they just touched the hem of His *garment*, and they were healed!

Then in Mark's Gospel, we read that the woman with the issue of blood ". . . *came in the press behind, and touched his [Jesus'] garment*" (Mark 5:27). Well, evidently, Jesus' garment became charged with that same power or anointing with which He Himself was anointed.

Also, the cloths that Paul laid hands upon became charged with the same anointing that Paul was anointed with, which was the healing and delivering power of God (Acts 19:11,12).

Then it seems that the healing power of God can be absorbed by certain materials, namely cloths. And that healing power or anointing can be transmitted or transferred from the clothes into the bodies of the sick.

The anointing is also measurable. We read in the Old Testament that God commanded the prophet Elijah to anoint Elisha to take his place, and it says Elisha asked for a double portion of Elijah's anointing (2 Kings 2:9).

Then in the Gospels we saw that Jesus was anointed to minister as He walked upon the earth. And John

3:34 says that Jesus had the anointing *without measure.*

The anointing is also *tangible.* The word "tangible" means *perceptible to the touch.* In other words, something that is tangible is capable of being touched.

For example, we know that the anointing that went into the woman with the issue of blood in Mark chapter 5 was tangible because Jesus knew *immediately* when that power went out of Him. Jesus was aware of an *outflow* of that healing power, and the woman was aware of the *reception* of that power. So the power had to have been tangible.

Ways the Anointing Is Transferred

Now that we've looked at the characteristics of the healing anointing, I want to focus on the ways it is transferred. One way is by the laying on of hands.

In His own ministry, Jesus used many methods in ministering to the sick. Sometimes He just said, "Arise and walk," and they arose and walked. But one of the main ways He ministered healing was by the laying on of hands.

For example, in Mark chapter 5, Jesus laid hands on Jairus' daughter, and she was healed. All through the New Testament, there are a number of instances where Jesus laid His hands on the sick and they were healed. The contact of His hands with the sick one permitted the healing anointing, or the power of God in Him, to flow into the sick one.

The healing anointing can also be transferred, as I mentioned earlier, through a cloth, such as a garment or handkerchief.

In Mark chapter 5, the woman with the issue of blood touched Jesus' clothes and found the power of God emanating from His Person. The Apostle Paul, knowing this same law of contact and transmission that governed the operation of the Spirit of God in healing, laid his hands on cloths or handkerchiefs (Acts 19:11,12). Those cloths were taken to the sick, and the diseases departed from them.

Some people in modern times might think that the transfer of the anointing through cloth is only superstition. But it's not superstition; it's a viable fact. It happened just the way the Word of God said it happened.

In other words, the healing anointing, emanating from Paul, transformed those handkerchiefs into "storage batteries" of Holy Ghost power. When they were laid on the sick, they charged the body with the healing anointing, and the diseases departed from them.

Healing Anointing vs. Ministry Anointing

As I said at the beginning of this lesson, the anointing for ministry automatically comes with the calling to stand in whatever office God has called you to. But the *healing anointing* is something different and separate from a *ministry anointing*.

For instance, Jesus said to me when He appeared to me in the vision in Rockwall, Texas, in 1950: "I have called you before you were born. I separated you from your mother's womb. Satan tried to destroy your life before you were born and many times since then, but My angels have watched over you and cared for you until this present hour."

Well, when Jesus said, "I have called you," that didn't mean He called me on that very day, September 2, 1950. He had called me to the ministry before I was born. I understood what He meant when He said, "I have called you."

After Jesus said, "I have called you," He said, "and I have anointed you." Well, again, I knew He wasn't talking about anointing me for the ministry that very day. No, the anointing came with the calling, and I'd already been ministering with that anointing for many years.

But when Jesus said to me, "And I have given unto you a *special* anointing to lay hands on the sick," I knew He was talking about giving me a *special* anointing on that very day, September 2, 1950.

Now I had been laying hands on the sick for years and had seen them healed. But I wasn't ministering with a special anointing; I was just ministering to the sick through the laying on of hands according to the Word of God.

After Jesus gave me a special anointing in that vision to lay hands on the sick, He said to me, among other things, "This special anointing will not work for you unless you tell the people exactly what I've told you; that is, tell them you saw Me. Tell them I spoke to you, and that I laid the finger of My right hand in the palm of each of your hands. Tell them that the anointing is in your hands. Tell them exactly what I've told you. And tell them if they'll *believe* it — that you're anointed — and *receive* it, then that power will flow from your hands into their body, and will undo what Satan has wrought. It will effect a healing and a cure therein."

Now, the laying on of hands isn't the only way to minister, but it's one way. And it's a scriptural way.

Laying on of hands is a point of contact that releases the healing power. Sometimes the healing power of God is ministered to a sick person to the degree that he is manifestly charged with the power of God, just like a person might be charged with electricity. Yet no real or final healing takes place until something happens that releases the faith of the individual.

Healing Is by Degree

We need to understand that healing is by degree. And the degree of healing is determined by two conditions. Number one, *the degree of healing power administered to the body.* A person can be less anointed or more anointed to minister healing just like a preacher can be less anointed or more anointed to preach.

In the same way, a person can be less anointed or more anointed with the healing anointing. I've noticed that when the anointing upon me is manifested in a greater degree, we have more healings take place in the service.

The second condition that determines the degree of healing is *the degree of faith released by the individual to give action to that healing power.*

You can see this in Mark chapter 5, in the case with the woman with the issue of blood. Jesus said, "... *Daughter, thy faith hath made thee whole. . .* " (v. 34). Someone might say, "I thought it was the power that flowed out of Jesus that made her whole." Yes, it was. *But it was her faith that gave action to that power.*

Jesus Christ and the Apostle Paul revealed and applied the laws that govern the operation of the healing anointing — the power of God. They demonstrated that the healing power of God is a tangible, transmittable, and measurable substance.

What was the power that flowed from Jesus' hands or was stored in His garments? Was it power that was inherent in Him as the Son of God? No. Acts 10:38 says, "... *God anointed Jesus of Nazareth with the HOLY GHOST and POWER: who went about doing good, and healing all that were oppressed of the devil. . . .*"

Where did that power come from? It came from God. And that same power — the healing power of God — is available today.

✳

Memory Text:

"... *God anointed Jesus of Nazareth with the Holy Ghost and with power: who went about doing good, and healing all that were oppressed of the devil; for God was with him*"

(Acts 10:38)

About the Author

Kenneth E. Hagin ministered for almost 70 years after God miraculously healed him of a deformed heart and an incurable blood disease at the age of 17. Even though Rev. Hagin went home to be with the Lord in 2003, the ministry he founded continues to bless multitudes around the globe.

Kenneth Hagin Ministries' radio program, *Rhema for Today*, is heard on more than 150 stations nationwide and on the Internet worldwide. Other outreaches include *The Word of Faith*, a free monthly magazine; crusades conducted throughout the nation; RHEMA Correspondence Bible School; RHEMA Bible Training Center; RHEMA Alumni Association; RHEMA Ministerial Association International; RHEMA Supportive Ministries Association; and the RHEMA Prison Ministry.

God has a *specific* plan for your life.
Are you ready?
RHEMA Bible Training Center

∞ Take your place in the Body of Christ for the last great revival.

∞ Learn to rightly divide God's Word and to hear His voice clearly.

∞ Discover how to be a willing vessel for God's glory.

∞ Receive practical hands-on ministry training from experienced ministers.

*Qualified instructors are waiting to teach, train,
and help **you** fulfill your destiny!*

Call today for information or application material.
1-888-28-FAITH (1-888-283-2484)
Offer #BK074:PRMDRBTC

www.rbtc.org

RHEMA Bible Training Center admits students of any race, color, or ethnic origin.

RHEMA

Correspondence Bible School

The RHEMA Correspondence Bible School is a home Bible study course that can help you in your everyday life!

This course of study has been designed with you in mind, providing practical teaching on prayer, faith, healing, Spirit-led living, and much more to help you live a victorious Christian life!

Flexible

Enroll any time: choose your topic of study; study at your own pace!

Affordable

Pay as you go—only $25 per lesson!

(Price subject to change without notice.)

Profitable

"Words cannot adequately describe the tremendous impact RCBS has had on my life. I have learned so much, and I am always sharing my newfound knowledge with everyone I can. I feel like a blind person who has just had his eyes opened!"

Louisiana

"RCBS has been a stepping-stone in my growing faith to serve God with the authority that He has given the Church over all the power of the enemy!"

New York